W9-BOB-442

How to Train Your

Shetland Sheepdog

liz palika

Photo by Isabelle Francais

SHETLAND SHEEPDOG

Photos by the author unless
otherwise credited.

The publisher would like to thank all of the owners of dogs pictured in this book, including the following: Bob Anderson, Karan J. Aurelius, Leslie Auwerter, Judy Charlton, Joanne Chaplele, Kathleen Collins, Kathy Dziegiel, Connie Fleming, John J. Gorman, Shirley Hardesty, Vickie Hill, L. Leeman, Sherry Lee, Mary MacDonald, Karen E. Manchester, Joyce L. Marciano, Sandra Myers, Laura Rodriguez, Marguerite Salls, Francisco Tejeda, Shirley Vicchitto, Elaine Wishnow, Linda Zimmerman

© T.F.H. Publications, Inc.

Distributed in the UNITED STATES to the Pet Trade by T.F.H. Publications, Inc., 1 TFH Plaza, Neptune City, NJ 07753; on the Internet at www.tfh.com; in CANADA by Rolf C. Hagen Inc., 3225 Sartelon St., Montreal, Quebec H4R 1E8; Pet Trade by H & L Pet Supplies Inc., 27 Kingston Crescent, Kitchener, Ontario N2B 2T6; in ENGLAND by T.F.H. Publications, PO Box 74, Havant PO9 5TT; in AUSTRALIA AND THE SOUTH PACIFIC by T.F.H. (Australia), Pty. Ltd., Box 149, Brookvale 2100 N.S.W., Australia; in NEW ZEALAND by Brooklands Aquarium Ltd., 5 McGiven Drive, New Plymouth, RD1 New Zealand; in SOUTH AFRICA by Rolf C. Hagen S.A. (PTY.) LTD., P.O. Box 201199, Durban North 4016, South Africa; in JAPAN by T.F.H. Publications, Japan—Jiro Tsuda, 10-12-3 Ohjidai, Sakura, Chiba 285, Japan. Published by T.F.H. Publications, Inc. MANUFACTURED IN THE UNITED STATES OF AMERICA BY T.F.H. PUBLICATIONS, INC.

Contents

INTRODUCTION

A good friend of mine, Lynda Miller, who has since passed away, loved Shelties. She showed her Shelties in conformation competition and obedience trials and participated in herding clinics. Her Shelties were her friends, companions, and pride and joy.

When I first met Lynda, I had German Shepherds, and I'll admit I didn't see the appeal of her breed. After all, they were so little! However, as I got to know Lynda and her dogs, I realized Shelties may be little,

but they don't know it. Every Sheltie has the heart of a big dog and a "go get 'em" attitude.

I have been teaching dog training classes since the mid-1970s and through the years, many breeds have come and gone as far as popularity goes. German Shepherds were very popular for a while, as were Rottweilers. Poodles of all sizes have been popular, as have Cocker Spaniels and Dachshunds. All along though, Shelties have maintained a core of popularity. They have never

Owners of Shelties love them for their big hearts, intelligence, and "go get 'em" attitude.

Photo by Isabelle Francais

shetland sheepdog

Shelties are wonderful dogs, but they aren't right for everyone. Choosing a dog to add to the family requires careful research.

Photo by Isabelle Francais

been the number-one most popular breed, but people who like Shelties really, really like them and often have more than one.

However, a Sheltie isn't the right dog for everyone. Shelties do need regular grooming and they shed, sometimes a lot. They can be barkers, which can cause problems with neighbors, especially in apartments and condos. Shelties are also very active dogs that need regular exercise. They are intelligent dogs with a strong work ethic and need something to do—something to keep their mind active.

Prospective dog owners need to know what a Sheltie is (and isn't) so that they make the right choice when adding a dog to the family. In this book I have tried to present Shetland Sheepdog owners (and prospective owners) with information about picking the right dog for their situation and how to make that dog a well-behaved member of the family.

Shelties are bright, intelligent dogs that love to work and want to please their owners when they understand what is expected of them. With training and help from their owner, they can be wonderful friends, partners, and companions.

SELECTING
the Right Dog for You

WHAT ARE SHETLAND SHEEPDOGS?

Shetland Sheepdogs (or, as they are commonly known, Shelties) originated in the Shetland Islands of Scotland. Dogs of a Border Collie type were brought to the islands to help with livestock on the rough, rocky subsistence farms. These strong herding dogs were bred to local small, intelligent, longer-coated dogs already in residence on the farms. Subsequent mixes with rough-coated Collies brought about the Shelties' Collie-like appearance.

Life was hard on these farms. The harsh climate and rough terrain made survival difficult and, in order to survive, the species living on the islands had to evolve. Over many generations, the animals surviving on the islands became smaller, which made them better able to handle the rough terrain and harsh climate, and hardier, which meant they were less likely to suffer injury and better able to stave off disease.

The Sheltie's strong build and hardy nature enabled the breed to thrive as a herding dog in the harsh climate of the Shetland Islands.

Photo by Isabelle Francais

shetland sheepdog

Photo by Isabelle Francais

The Shetland Sheepdog looks like a Collie in miniature. At about 15 inches tall, a Sheltie is small enough to be cuddled.

A good example of this evolution is the Shetland pony. Shetland ponies are much smaller than their equine cousins; yet are known for their strong build, hardy nature, and go get 'em attitude. A small, hardy horse required less food and pasture land and was better able to withstand the extremes of weather. This evolution affected all the animals on the islands, including cattle, goats, and the dog that would eventually become the Shetland Sheepdog.

However, the mixture of several different breeds and types of dog made it difficult to standardize the size and look (or type) of the early Shelties. *The Complete Dog Book,* by the American Kennel Club (AKC), says of the breed's history, "The Shetland Sheepdog Club of the Shetland Islands (formed in 1908) wanted the breed to look like a rough Collie in miniature; not more than 15 inches tall at the shoulder. The Scottish Shetland Sheepdog Club wanted the breed to look like a modern show Collie in miniature, with an ideal height of 12 inches." Various other clubs had their own ideal picture (and size) of a Sheltie, but eventually the newest club, the American Shetland Sheepdog Association, said that the ideal Sheltie would be between 13 and 16 inches tall at the shoulder while maintaining the look of a Collie in miniature.

During the early 1900s, while breeders were attempting to standardize a Sheltie type, crosses with modern Collies were made. This helped create the lovely Sheltie head, which looks so much like a smaller version of the Collie, with the correct ears and ear set, as well as the lovely Collie and Sheltie expression. This cross also gave the modern Sheltie the Collie's

Photo by Isabelle Francais

Although today most are far removed from their origin as working dogs, Shelties retain their long, water-resistant coats.

beautiful, weather-resistant coat.

Today, Shelties are no longer crossed with Collies. Breeders try to create the perfect Sheltie (according to the written description of the breed—the standard) by breeding together only those dogs and bitches that will perpetuate the best attributes of the breed. The American Kennel Club's standard for the Shetland Sheepdog says that the ideal Sheltie should be between 13 and 16 inches tall at the shoulder, with weight appropriate to height. The head should be wedge-shaped, tapering slightly from ears to nose. The eyes are almond-shaped and dark. The ears are small, placed high on the skull, and carried erect with the tips folding forward.

Shelties have a double coat, which means the lovely long outer coat has a thick furry undercoat. The coat on the head, ears, feet, and forelegs is short and smooth. Colors range from black, blue merle, and a deep, dark mahogany to a golden brown. White markings on the muzzle, including a blaze between the eyes, are permissible, as are white markings on the neck ruff and legs and feet.

As a herding dog, the Sheltie must show the ability to cover ground in a smooth, effortless trot. Even as a small dog, the Sheltie should give the impression of strength, agility, and ability to do the job it was meant to do—herd livestock. The modern Shetland Sheepdog is a beautiful dog with a gorgeous coat, attractive coloring and markings, the expression of a Collie in miniature, and personality and charm.

Temperament

Herding dogs must be able to work with their owner or shepherd, must be easily trained, and have a strong desire to work and work hard. The life of a livestock herding dog is not easy. It means

Photo by Isabelle Francais

This Sheltie's markings represent the most familiar color pattern, although according to the breed standard, many colors are permissible.

shetland sheepdog

working in all weather—cold, hot, windy, snowing, or worse—because often the livestock need help most when the weather threatens. A herding dog can't quit working because of bad weather. Herding dogs face danger every day, from angry mother cows or sheep to predators, brambles, thorns, or snakes. The herding dog must be loyal, both to its livestock charges and to its owner or shepherd.

Shelties have all of these traits. Because of the breed's easy trainability and its strong desire to work, it is a wonderful and high-scoring obedience competition dog. The breed's loving, gentle nature has made it a favorite companion dog and therapy dog. The breed's athletic abilities have made it possible for the dog to participate in dog sports, including flyball and agility. Many Sheltie owners participate in herding competitions and trials to showcase the breed's ancient herding instincts.

Shetland Sheepdogs are affectionate, playful, and very people-oriented and need to spend time with their owners. In fact, a Sheltie left alone too much can easily become a problem barker. Shelties are not good dogs to be left alone in the backyard all day.

Benjamin L. Hart, DVM, and Lynette A. Hart, authors of *The Perfect Puppy,* say that Shelties

A herding dog's work is never done! Shelties have a strong desire to work hard and please their owners, making them ideal for advanced training.

Photo by Tara Darling

shetland sheepdog

Shetland Sheepdogs are affectionate and people-oriented. They love to spend time with their families.

are easy to housetrain, easy to obedience train, and very affectionate and playful. Shelties are very active dogs and need regular exercise. On the downside, Shelties can be problem barkers and in stressful situations can be snappy, especially toward small children. The authors say, "According to our authorities, excessive barking is not a trait that can be suppressed by selecting a certain sex, but snapping at children will likely occur a little less with a female." They continue, "The Sheltie would make a fine family pet, especially if introduced when the children are old enough not to provoke snapping."

With their herding heritage, Shelties are very alert, watchful, and protective. Shelties watch everything: the mail carrier, the kids next door, the meter reader, and every butterfly that flies through the yard. Most Shelties will bark when people approach the house, and although this watchfulness is usually a desirable trait, Shelties need to be taught how much barking is appropriate and when to stop.

A well-trained, well-socialized Sheltie is a wonderful companion. However, that training and socialization is necessary for all Shelties. The breed's intelligence, alertness, and watchful personality can—without training and socialization—make the breed a nuisance. Fearfulness and shyness can result from poor breeding practices or inadequate socialization. Problem barking can be the result of a lack of training, poor socialization, or too much time spent home alone. Before adding a Sheltie to your family, make sure this is the right breed for you.

IS A SHELTIE THE RIGHT DOG FOR YOU?

Evaluating Your Personality and Lifestyle

The decision to add a dog to your family is not a decision to be made on impulse. Granted, Shelties are cute little dogs, and puppies are absolutely adorable, but Shelties are not the right dog for every family. This is a 14- to 16-year commitment—let's make sure a Sheltie is the right dog for you.

Don't assume that getting a Sheltie requires raising a dog from puppyhood. In many situations, your best choice might be an older dog. Do you come home from work tired but then like to get outside, walking or riding your bicycle?

If so, perhaps an adult dog from a Sheltie rescue organization or shelter might suit your needs. Do you work at home, have short work hours, and enjoy doing things? In that case, either a puppy or an active young dog might please you.

Are you retired and live alone? If so, and your health is good, a puppy will keep you busy and active. Are there active children in your household? Shelties can be wonderful with kids when raised with them; however, an adult dog that has not lived with kids should not be adopted into a family with young, active children.

Do you work long hours, come home tired, and then just want to relax, spending the evening reading or watching television? If you do, a Sheltie is not the right dog for you unless you're willing to adopt an older Sheltie from a rescue group. (Even then, most Shelties do not do well alone for many hours each day.)

Being the center of a dog's universe can be thrilling to some people and overwhelming to others. If you don't like being followed, watched, or touched, don't get a Shetland Sheepdog! A Sheltie will follow you from room to room and will be

Photo by Isabelle Francais

A Sheltie that has grown up around children is a better choice for a young family than an adult dog that has not lived with kids.

heartbroken if you even go to the bathroom without him. When you sit down, the Sheltie will want to cuddle close to you or lie on your feet. When you leave the house, the Sheltie will want to go with you. Obviously, having a dog with you for 24 hours a day is impossible for most people. However, if you own a Sheltie, you will need to provide as much companionship as possible.

The Sheltie's Needs

Before you add a Sheltie to your family, make sure you can fulfill the dog's needs. First of all, as has been mentioned earlier, your time and companionship is very important to a Sheltie. Shelties do very poorly alone in a backyard all day. This is a companion breed that needs to spend time with you.

You will also have to have a very secure fence around your yard. As a protective herding dog, Shelties have been known to charge at and chase people walking down the sidewalk in front of their house. This natural trait is okay when the dog is working sheep—after all, it needed to protect the sheep from predators. However, in today's world a dog that chases people is considered dangerous!

Shelties do require regular

daily exercise. If you're a jogger and can take your dog jogging with you, this will work well. You may also want to teach your Sheltie to run alongside your bicycle or run with you while you rollerblade. A young, healthy Shetland Sheepdog is not a couch potato.

Shelties also require regular grooming. The long, weather-resistant double coat requires daily maintenance to keep it healthy. Twice each year (spring and fall) Shelties shed, and when they shed, they shed a *lot*. Regular brushing, combing, and bathing will keep the hair in your house to a minimum, but that grooming must be done on a regular basis. A Sheltie that is

not groomed regularly will smell, mat (the coat will tangle in knots), develop skin problems under the dirty matted coat, and could even suffer from health problems.

SELECTING THE RIGHT DOG

Male or Female?

There are a lot of myths concerning the personality traits of both males and females. Although there are a few traits that are related to the sexes, ultimately it depends more on the personality of the individual dog.

Female Shelties are usually a little more tolerant of children,

These seven-week-old Sheltie puppies are awfully cute, but a wise potential owner knows how much time and care they will require.

Photo by Isabelle Francais

shetland sheepdog

All Shelties need to be groomed regularly—an important consideration when deciding if this is the right dog for you. Your local pet shop sells excellent grooming supplies, which can sometimes be purchased in affordable combination packages. Photo courtesy of Wahl, USA.

especially younger kids who may behave inappropriately around the dog.

Male Shelties are usually a little bigger and often have a heavier coat that will need more grooming. Male Shelties may be a little more protective.

Spayed and neutered bitches (females) and dogs (males) are usually a little calmer than those that are not; spaying and neutering removes the sexual hormones and, as a result, the sexual tension that can accompany those hormones. To be a good pet, your Sheltie doesn't need those hormones anyway.

MONEY MATTERS

Do you have the financial means to care for a dog? Good-quality food is not inexpensive, and buying dog food is one of those times when you get what you pay for—inexpensive food is not good nutrition for your dog. Veterinary care is not cheap, either, but it is a necessity. Your dog will need vaccinations and regular checkups and will need to be spayed or neutered. You will need grooming supplies, including brushes, combs, nail clippers, and flea and tick control products. Your dog will need a collar and leash and a kennel crate. You will need to invest in a dog training class (or two!). Also, at some point during your dog's life, there may be an emergency veterinary call because of an injury or illness. You will need the financial resources to care for your dog and must never delay needed care because of a lack of money.

What Age?

Puppies are adorable, especially little Sheltie puppies. These tiny little fluffballs are *so* cute. However, adding a puppy to your life is just like adding a new baby to the family. In fact, raising a puppy is much like raising a child, except that the puppy will grow up faster. As the puppy learns and grows, it will become a vital part of your family, and by the time your puppy has grown up (at about two years of age), your young Shetland Sheepdog will have become a good friend.

However, it takes a lot of work to raise a puppy, and for many people, adding a puppy to their lives may not be the right choice. But that doesn't mean these people can't have a dog. There are many Shelties that need homes, and these dogs could be just the answer for people who do not have the time to spend raising a puppy.

With an adult dog, many of your questions have already been answered. You know how big the dog is going to be because he's already grown up. You know how much coat care he will need because he already has his adult coat. You can get to know his personality, you can see what training he's had (or not had) and you can look at his state of health. With a puppy, many of these things are unknown until the puppy grows up.

There are some drawbacks to adopting an adult dog. Adopting an adult can be compared to buying a used car; sometimes you get a gem, sometimes you get a lemon. You don't know how the dog has been treated prior to your

Photo by Isabelle Francais

Adopting an adult Sheltie is a great idea for a busy or less active owner. Give your new adult dog plenty of time to adjust to his new home.

adopting him, and these unknowns can affect his future behavior. Many times, too, his past health care is unknown. Newly adopted dogs must also be given time to settle into their new home. Emotional and physical adjustments take time.

Finding an Adult Dog

Occasionally, Shelties are given up by their owners, and these dogs are often available for adoption. Sometimes people get a Sheltie without having researched the breed and give the dog up because they can't deal with the coat care or the breed's activity level. Perhaps the dog's owner passed away and other family members cannot take the dog. Dogs can be given up by their owners for any number of reasons. Check for these dogs at your local humane society or animal shelter.

Evaluating an Adult Dog

Once you have found an adult Sheltie you like, how do you decide if this is the right dog for you? Emotions certainly play a part in this decision—do you like the dog? There is more of a chance of success in this new relationship if you and the dog like each other. However, there is more to the decision-making process than just this.

Do you know why the dog was given up by its first owners? Sometimes a dog loses its home through no fault of its own— perhaps the owner was transferred overseas or passed away. However, if the dog was given up because of behavior problems, you need to know that.

The most common behavior problem in Shelties is barking. A problem barker can cause discontent in the family and the neighborhood. Before you adopt the dog, make sure this dog doesn't have a barking problem.

RESCUE GROUPS

Many breed clubs sponsor or run breed rescue groups. These groups screen and evaluate all of the dogs they process. Dogs are checked for personality or temperament flaws (such as shyness, fearfulness, or aggression). Dogs are also evaluated as to how much (or how little) training they have had. The dogs are spayed or neutered, vaccinated, any health problems are identified, and treatment is begun. This screening process can be invaluable to the potential adopter. To find a Sheltie rescue group near you, call your local humane society or shelter.

When you find an adult dog you like, make sure that you can live with any behavior problems he may exhibit until he has been better trained.

Photo by Isabelle Francais

shetland sheepdog

Photo by Isabelle Francais

Each puppy is different. Try to choose one with a personality that matches yours.

What do you know of the dog's previous life? Has he had any obedience training? Is he housetrained? These are important issues, because even if you are willing to give the dog some obedience training, housetraining a previously untrained dog can be quite an undertaking.

What is the dog's personality like? When you whistle or speak to the dog, does he look at you happily, wagging his tail? If he does, great. If he looks sideways at you, slinks, or bares his teeth, be careful. He could be worried or afraid because of previous mistreatment, but an unknown fearful dog might also bite.

Ideally, you want a Sheltie that is happy to see you without showing too much worry or fear. You want a dog that is housetrained, is not a problem barker, and has had at least some obedience training. Make sure that any behavior problems are ones that you can live with for the time being and are willing to work on in the future. Ideally, too, the dog has been vaccinated and either spayed or neutered.

Finding a Puppy

If you have the time, resources, and patience to raise a puppy, you will want to find a reputable breeder. Breeder referrals can come from many sources. People walking their dog might refer you to their breeder. A veterinarian, groomer, or trainer might know of some reputable breeders. Many of the national dog magazines have advertisements and classified ads. You might also want to attend a dog show in your community and talk to people attending the show.

Once you find a few breeders, call and set up an appointment to talk to them. At your meeting, ask the breeders a few questions: "Are you active in the dog world?" This answer will tell you many things. First, if the breeder shows her dogs in conformation dog shows, her Shelties are probably good examples of the breed. If she competes in obedience trials, her dogs are trainable. If she participates in herding trials, her dogs have the working instincts Shelties should have.

"Do you belong to any of the national or regional Sheltie clubs?" Breeders who do are more likely to be up-to-date on happenings within the breed, including information about genetics or health problems.

"What health problems have you seen in your dogs?" If the breeder says none, be skeptical. A line with no health problems is rare. Shelties can have a number of different health problems, including eye disorders, allergies, and epilepsy. Reputable breeders should be honest with you about potential health problems and what they are doing to try and prevent these problems.

"Can you provide me with a list of references?" Although this list will be of people the breeder thinks will give good references, it is still helpful to you. You can ask about their experience with the breeder— "Did the breeder work well with you?" "Would you buy another puppy from her?"

Caring breeders will ask you as many questions as you ask them. They want to know that you are the right person for their dogs. Don't get defensive—the breeder is trying to do the right thing. Instead, answer the questions honestly. If by some chance the breeder says that her dogs are not right for you, listen to her—she knows her dogs best. Perhaps her dogs are too active for your lifestyle or perhaps her dogs all like to bark and you live in a condo. She may be right.

Evaluating a Puppy

Each puppy has his or her own personality, and finding the right personality to match with yours is sometimes a challenge. For example, if you are outgoing, extroverted, and active, a quiet, withdrawn, submissive puppy would be terrified in your household. You will need a puppy more like you. On the other hand, that quiet puppy would probably do very well for a quiet person or a less active retiree.

When you go to look at a litter of puppies, there are a few things you can do to help evaluate the puppy's personality. First, with a puppy away from his mother and littermates, place him on the ground and walk a few steps away. Squat down and call the puppy. An outgoing, extroverted Sheltie will come happily and try to climb into your lap. If you stand up and walk away, the extrovert will follow you, trying to get underfoot. If you crumple up a piece of paper and throw it a few feet away, the extrovert will dash after it and bring it back proudly. This Sheltie will do best in an active home. He will need lots of exercise, training, and a job to keep his mind busy.

Your Sheltie will be a cherished family member for many years— don't rush this important decision.

BE CAREFUL

Adding a dog to your family should be a time of anticipation and excitement, but it also requires thought, self-analysis, and research. Hopefully, this dog will be a treasured companion for the next 14 to 16 years. Take the time to make this decision wisely.

A quiet, submissive puppy will come to you when you call but may do a belly crawl or may roll over and bare his belly. When you get up to walk away, he will watch you but may be hesitant to follow. If you toss the paper, he may go after it and even bring it part of the way back but may be hesitant to bring it all the way to you. This puppy will need a quiet owner, gentle handling, and positive training to build up his confidence.

These two puppies are the extremes. Most Shelties are somewhere in between these two personality types. Try to find a puppy with a personality that will be comfortable with yours. Don't bring home an active puppy if you have a sedate personality. Don't get a puppy in the hopes of changing his personality—that doesn't work and will only result in stress and discord in your relationship.

shetland sheepdog

Canine DEVELOPMENT Stages

UNDERSTANDING THE DOG-OWNER BOND

Experts now feel that dogs were first domesticated as much as 135,000 years ago. Early cavemen and women could have conceivably shared their caves and fires with the ancestors of today's dogs. In spite of this long, shared history, the bond that we have with dogs must be renewed with each puppy. The bond itself is not hereditary, although the tendency to bond is; this relationship is what makes owning a dog so special. To understand when and how this bond develops, it's important to understand that your Shetland Sheepdog is a dog, not a person in a fuzzy dog suit.

Families and Packs

Most researchers agree that the ancestors of today's dogs were wolves. They disagree on which wolves those ancestors were—either the ancestors to today's gray wolves or a species of wolf that is now extinct. In any event, wolves are social creatures that live in an extended family pack. The pack might consist of a dominant (alpha) male and a dominant (alpha) female, and these two are usually the only two that breed. There will also be subordinate males and females, juveniles, and puppies. This is a very harmonious group that hunts together, plays together, defends its territory against intruders, and cares for each other. The only discord occurs when there is a change in the pack order. If one of the leaders becomes disabled, an adult leaves the pack, or a

The bond between a Sheltie and his owner can never be broken.

Photo by Isabelle Francais

subordinate adult tries to assume dominance, there may be some jockeying around to fill that position.

Many experts feel domesticated dogs adapt so well to our lifestyle because we also live in groups. We call our groups families instead of packs, but they are still social groups. However, the comparison isn't really accurate; our families are much more chaotic than the average wolf pack! We are terribly inconsistent with our social rules and rules for behavior. (We let our Sheltie jump up and paw us when we're in grubby clothes but yell at him when he jumps up on our good clothes!) To the dog, our communication skills are also confusing; our voice says one thing while our body language says something else. To our dogs, we are very complex, confusing creatures. We can say that both dogs and humans live in social groups, and we can use that comparison to understand a little more about our dogs. However, we must also understand our families are very different from a wolf pack.

FROM BIRTH TO FOUR WEEKS OF AGE

For the first three weeks of life, the family and the pack are unimportant as far as the Sheltie puppy is concerned. The only one of any significance is his mother. She is the key to his survival and the source of food, warmth, and security.

Dogs, like their ancestors the wolves, naturally live in packs. Your pet Sheltie's pack is his human family.

Photo by Isabelle Francais

shetland sheepdog

Photo by Isabelle Francais

During the first few weeks of life, the mother dog is the key to a puppy's survival.

At four weeks of age, the puppy's needs are still being met by his mother, but his littermates are becoming more important. His brothers and sisters provide warmth and security when their mother leaves the nest. His curiosity is developing, and he will climb on and over his littermates, learning their scent and feel. During this period he will learn to use his sense of hearing to follow sounds and his sense of vision to follow moving objects. His mom will also start disciplining the puppies—very gently, of course—and this early discipline is vitally important to the puppies' future acceptance of discipline and training.

The breeder should be handling the puppies now to get them used to gentle handling by people. The puppies at this age can learn the difference between their mother's touch and a human touch.

WEEKS FIVE THROUGH SEVEN

The young Sheltie puppy goes through some tremendous changes between five and seven weeks of age. He is learning to recognize people and starting to respond to individual voices. He is playing more with his littermates, and the wrestling and scuffling teach each puppy how to get along, how to play, when the play is too rough, when to be submissive, and what to take seriously. His mother's discipline at this stage of development teaches the puppy to accept corrections.

The puppies should never be taken from their mother at this

Photo by Isabelle Francais

Gently handling young puppies teaches them to respond to humans without fear or aggression.

sent to new homes may have lasting behavior problems. They often have difficulty dealing with other dogs, may have trouble accepting rules and discipline, and may become excessively shy, aggressive, or fearful.

THE EIGHTH WEEK

The eighth week of life is a frightening time for most puppies. Puppies go through several fear periods during their growth, and this is the first one. Even though this is the traditional time for most puppies to go to their new homes, they would actually benefit by staying with their littermates for one more week. If the puppy leaves the breeder's home during this fear stage of development. Sheltie puppies taken away now and

The mother dog should be permitted to correct her puppies so that they learn to accept discipline.

Photo by Isabelle Francais

shetland sheepdog

period and is frightened by the car ride home, he may retain that fear of car rides for the rest of his life. In fact, this stress is why so many puppies get carsick. The same applies to the puppy's new home, his first trip to the veterinarian's office, and anything else that frightens him.

WEEKS NINE THROUGH TWELVE

The Sheltie puppy can go to his new home any time during the ninth and tenth weeks of life. At this age, he is ready to form permanent relationships. Take advantage of this and spend time with your new puppy, playing with him and encouraging him to explore his new world. Teach him his name by calling him in a happy, high-pitched tone of voice. Encourage him to follow you by backing away from him, patting your leg, and calling him to you.

Socialization is very important now, too. Socialization is more than simply introducing your puppy to other people, dogs, noises, and places. It is making sure your Sheltie puppy is not frightened by these things as you introduce them. For example, once your puppy has had some vaccinations (check with your veterinarian), take

LET THE MOTHER DOG CORRECT

Some inexperienced breeders will stop the mother dog from correcting her puppies, perhaps thinking that the mother dog is impatient, tired, or a poor mother. When the mother dog is not allowed to correct the puppies naturally, the puppies do not learn how to accept discipline and therefore have a hard time later when their new owner tries to establish some rules. Orphaned puppies raised by people suffer from the same problems. The mother dog knows instinctively what to do for her babies, and sometimes a correction—a low growl, a bark, or a snap of the teeth—is exactly what is needed.

your puppy with you to the pet store when you go to buy dog food. While there, introduce your puppy to the store clerks, other customers, and even to the store parrot. Your trip there could also include walking up some stairs, walking on slippery floors, and going through an automatic door. All of these things, introduced gradually and with encouragement and repeated all over town (on different days, of course), add up to a confident, well-socialized puppy.

During this stage of development, your puppy's

Your Sheltie puppy will need a nutritionally fortified diet geared toward his stage of life. Look for foods that are naturally preserved, contain no by-products, and are 100% guaranteed. Photo courtesy of Midwestern Pet Foods, Inc.

pack instincts are developing. He is beginning to understand which people belong to his pack or family and which do not. Do not let him growl at visitors during this stage—he is much too young to understand when and how to protect. Instead, stop the growling and let him know that you—as his pack leader—can protect the family.

You can show him his position in the family in several different ways, but one of the easiest is to lay him down, roll him over, and give him a tummy This exercise may seem very simple, but by baring his tummy he is assuming a submissive position to you. When his

As your puppy learns his place in your family "pack," he needs gentle reminders that you are the leader and will protect him.

Photo by Isabelle Francais

mother corrected him by growling or barking at him, he would roll over and bare his tummy to her, in essence telling her, "Okay! I understand, you're the boss!" When you have him roll over for a tummy rub, you are helping him understand the same message, but you are doing it in a very gentle, loving way.

During this stage of development, discipline is very important. Love, affection, and security are still important too, of course, but right now your Sheltie puppy needs to learn that his life is governed by some rules. Don't allow him to do anything now that you won't want him to continue doing later as a full-grown dog.

WEEKS THIRTEEN THROUGH SIXTEEN

From 13 through 16 weeks of age, your Sheltie puppy will be trying to establish his position in your family pack. If you were able to set some rules in earlier stages of development, this won't be quite so difficult. However, if you give in to that adorable fluffy puppy, this could be a challenging time!

Consistency in enforcing household rules is very important now, and everyone in the family or household should be enforcing the rules the same way. Shelties are very intelligent and perceptive, and if your puppy senses a weak link in the chain of command, he will take advantage of it. This

Learning to retrieve is a great physical and mental exercise for a young Sheltie.

Photo by Isabelle Francais

s h e t l a n d   s h e e p d o g

27

doesn't mean he's a bad puppy, it simply means he's a smart puppy!

Dominant personality puppies may start mounting behavior on small children in the family or on the puppy's toys. Obviously, this is undesirable behavior and should be stopped immediately. Just don't let it happen.

Socialization to other people, friendly dogs, and other experiences should continue throughout this stage of development.

WEEKS SEVENTEEN THROUGH TWENTY-SIX

Sometime between 17 and 26 weeks of age, most puppies go through another fear period, much like the one they went through at 8 weeks of age. Things the puppy had accepted as normal may suddenly become frightening. A friend's Shetland Sheepdog walked into the backyard and began barking fearfully at a potted plant that had been there in the same spot since before the puppy joined the family. It was if the puppy had never noticed it before, and all at once it was very scary!

Make sure you don't reinforce any of these fears. If

RETRIEVING

Begin retrieving games at 9 to 12 weeks of age. Get your Sheltie's attention with a toy he likes, and then toss it four to six feet away. When he grabs the toy, call him back to you in a happy tone of voice. Praise him enthusiastically when he brings it back to you. If he runs away and tries to get you to chase him, stand up and walk away, stopping the game completely. Don't chase him. Let him learn now, while he's young, that he must play games by your rules. Chasing a ball or soft flying disc can be great exercise for the puppy, and by teaching him to play by your rules, it also sets the stage for a sound working relationship later.

---

you pet him or cuddle him and tell him softly, "It's okay, sweetie, don't be afraid," he will assume this is positive reinforcement for his fears. In other words, your puppy will think he was right to be afraid. Instead, walk up to whatever is scaring him, letting him see you touch it, as you tell him, "Look at this!" Use a happy, fun, playful tone of voice so that he can see the thing he is afraid of really isn't scary at all.

Your Sheltie's protective instincts will continue to develop through this stage. If your puppy continues to show protectiveness or aggression (by growling, snarling, barking, or raising his hackles), interrupt his behavior by turning him away or distracting him. If you encourage this behavior this early, or if you correct it too harshly, you will put too much emphasis on it and your puppy may continue to do it. Too much emphasis this young may result in overprotectiveness or fearfulness in your dog as he grows up. Instead, react with calmness and just stop it from happening.

Shetland Sheepdogs are naturally protective as adults, and if you wanted a Sheltie for

If your young Sheltie growls or barks at strangers, calmly interrupt his behavior by turning him away or distracting him with a toy.

Photo by Isabelle Francais

this trait, don't worry about interrupting the behavior now. This training will not hamper those instincts. At this age, your puppy doesn't know what or when to protect. Instead of letting him take over (and learn bad habits), stop his behavior and let him know that you are in charge. Later, when he's more mature, you can encourage the specific protectiveness you want.

THE TEENAGE MONTHS

The teenage months in dogs are very much like the teenage years in human children. Human adolescents are feeling strong and striving to prove their ability to take care of themselves. They want to be independent, yet they still want the security of home. These two conflicting needs seem to drive some teens (and their parents) absolutely crazy.

Dogs can be very much the same way. Shelties in adolescence push the boundaries of their rules, trying to see if you really will enforce them. Most Sheltie owners say their dogs in this stage of growing up act "too full of themselves."

The teenage stage in Shelties usually hits at about nine

months of age, although it's not unusual to see it happen a month or two earlier. You'll know when it happens. One day you will ask your previously well-trained dog to do something he knows very well, such as sit, and he'll look at you as if you're nuts. He's never heard that word before in his life, and even if he had, he still wouldn't do it! Other common behaviors include a regression in social skills. Your previously well-socialized Sheltie may start barking at other dogs or jumping on people. He may start getting nippy with the children, or he may even start herding the cat.

During this stage of development, you really need to consistently enforce social and household rules. Hopefully, you will have already started obedience training, because that control will help. If you haven't started obedience training, do so now—don't wait any longer.

Make sure, too, that your dog regards you as the leader. This is not the time to try and be best friends—that would cause a dominant personality to regard you as weak. Instead, act like the leader. Stand tall when you relate to your dog. Bend over him (not down to him)

when you pet him. You should always go first through doorways or up the stairs— make him wait and follow you. Always eat first before you feed him.

As the leader, you can give him permission to do things. For example, if he goes to pick up a toy for you to throw for him, give him permission to do it, "Good boy to bring me your toy!" If he lies down at your feet (by his own choice) tell him, "Good boy to lie down!" By giving him permission and praising him, you are putting yourself in control, even though he was already doing it of his own accord.

When he's a teenager, your Sheltie may suddenly "forget" that he's not supposed to jump up on people. During this stage, you need to consistently reinforce household rules.

Photo by Isabelle Francais

You need to understand that this rebellion is not aimed at you, personally. Your Sheltie is not doing this to you. Instead, it is a very natural part of growing up. Keep in mind that this, too, shall pass. Your Sheltie will grow up someday. Adolescence usually only lasts a few months (in dogs, anyway).

GROWING UP

Shelties are not usually considered fully mature mentally and physically until they are two years old. And even then, some Shelties still behave like a puppy for even longer. Usually, the bitches (females) act mature a little earlier than the males.

After the teenage stage but before maturity, your Sheltie may go through another fear period. This usually hits at about 14 months of age, but it may be later. Handle this one just like you did the others— don't reinforce your dog's fears. Happily, this is usually the last fear stage your dog will have.

There may be another period of challenging—seeing if you really are the boss—at about 18 months of age. Treat this as you did the teenage stage: Enforce the rules and praise what he does right.

When your Sheltie reaches his second birthday, throw a party. He is usually considered grown up now.

At two years of age, Shelties, unlike human children, are all grown up!

Photo by Robert Pearcy

Early
PUPPY
Training

BLANK SLATE

A puppy's mind is like a newly formatted computer disk. What you teach your Sheltie puppy in his early months will have bearing on the puppy's behavior for the rest of his life. Therefore, it's important to keep in mind a vision of what your Sheltie will grow up to be. Although Shelties are small- to medium-sized dogs, they are active herding dogs. At 10 weeks of age, your Sheltie puppy will enjoy a cuddle on your lap, but will you still want him to do that when he's 25 pounds of hard muscle and long coat? Especially when he doesn't want to lie still but instead wants you to play? Teach him as a puppy what you want him to do as an adult.

HOUSETRAINING

One of the most common methods of housetraining a puppy is paper training. The puppy is taught to relieve himself on newspapers and then, at some point, is retrained to go outside. Paper training teaches the puppy to relieve himself in the house. Is that really what you want your Sheltie to know?

Teach your Sheltie what you want him to know now *and* later as an adult. Take him outside to the place where you want him to relieve himself and tell him, "Sweetie, go potty." (Use any word you'll be comfortable saying.) When he has done what it is he needs to do, praise him.

Don't just open the door and send your puppy outside. How do you know that he has relieved himself? Go out with him so that you can teach him the command, praise him when he does it, and know that he is done and it's safe to let him back inside.

Successful housetraining is based on setting your Sheltie puppy up for success rather than failure. Keep accidents to a minimum and praise him when he relieves himself in the correct location.

Establish a Routine

Shelties, like many other dogs, are creatures of habit and thrive on a routine. Housetraining is much easier if there is a set routine for eating, eliminating, playing, walking,

Photo by Isabelle Francais

A puppy's mind is a blank slate. Teach your Sheltie what you want him to know now and as an adult.

shetland sheepdog

training, and sleeping. A workable schedule might look like this:

• **6:00 am**—Dad wakes up and takes the puppy outside. After the puppy relieves himself, Dad praises him and brings him inside. Dad fixes the puppy's breakfast, offers him water, and then sends him out in the backyard while Dad goes to take his shower.

• **7:00 am**—Mom goes outside to play with the puppy for a few minutes before getting ready for work. Just before she leaves, she brings the puppy inside, puts him in his crate, and gives him a treat.

• **11:00 am**—A dog-loving neighbor who is retired comes over. He lets the puppy out of his crate and takes him outside. The neighbor is familiar with the puppy's training, so he praises the puppy when he relieves himself. He throws the ball for the puppy, pets him, and cuddles him. When the puppy is worn out, he puts him back in his crate and gives him a treat.

• **3:00 pm**—Daughter comes home from school and takes the puppy outside. She throws the ball for the puppy, cleans up the yard a little, and then takes the puppy for a walk. When they get back, she brings

> ### PUNISHMENT
> Do not try to housetrain your puppy by correcting him for relieving himself in the house. If you scold him or rub his nose in his mess, you are not teaching him where he needs to relieve himself; you are, instead, teaching him that you think going potty is wrong. Because he has to go, he will then become sneaky about it, and you will find puddles and piles in strange places. Keep in mind that the act of relieving himself is very natural—he *has* to do it. Instead of concentrating on correction, emphasize the praise for going in the right place.

Asking a neighbor or professional petsitter to assist with your puppy's housetraining during the day may help speed up the process.

Photo by Isabelle Francais

the puppy inside to her bedroom while she does her homework.

• **6:00 pm**—Mom takes the puppy outside to go potty, praises him, and then feeds him dinner.

• **8:00 pm**—After Daughter plays with the puppy, she brushes him and then takes him outside to go potty.

• **11:00 pm**—Dad takes the puppy outside for one last trip before bed.

The schedule you set up will have to work with your normal routine and lifestyle. Just keep in mind that your Sheltie puppy should not remain in the crate

Never keep your Sheltie in his crate for longer than four hours at a time, except at night.

Photo by Isabelle Francais

THERE ARE NO ACCIDENTS
If the puppy relieves himself in the house, it is not his fault, it's yours. That means the puppy was not supervised well enough or he wasn't taken outside in time. The act of relieving himself is very natural to the puppy, and the idea that there are certain areas where it is not acceptable is foreign. His instincts tell him to keep his bed clean, but that's all. You need to teach him where you want him to go and to prevent him from going in other places. That requires your supervision.

for longer than three to four hours at a time, except during the night. In addition, the puppy will need to relieve himself after waking up, eating, and playtime, and every three to four hours in between.

Limit the Puppy's Freedom
Many puppies do not want to take the time to go outside to relieve themselves because everything exciting happens in the house. After all, that's where all the family members are. If your Sheltie puppy is like this, you will find him sneaking off somewhere—behind the sofa or to another room—to relieve himself. By limiting the puppy's freedom you can

PATIENCE, PATIENCE, AND MORE PATIENCE

Sheltie puppies need time to develop bowel and bladder control. Establish a routine that seems to work well for you and your puppy and then stick to it. Give your puppy time to learn what you want and time to grow up. If you stick to the schedule, your puppy will progress. However, don't let success go to your head. A few weeks without a mistake doesn't mean your Sheltie puppy is housetrained, it means your routine is working! Too much freedom too soon will result in problems.

prevent some of these mistakes. Close bedroom doors and use baby gates across hallways to keep him close. If you can't keep an eye on him, put him in his crate or outside.

CRATE TRAINING

By about five weeks of age, most puppies are starting to toddle away from their mom and littermates to relieve themselves. You can use this instinct to keep the bed clean to your advantage, and with the help of a crate, you can housetrain your Sheltie puppy.

A crate is not a doggie prison. Even adult dogs love to curl up in small, dark places, and many voluntarily sleep in their crates.

Photo by Isabelle Francais

shetland sheepdog

A crate is a plastic or wire travel cage that you can use as your Sheltie's bed. Many new Sheltie owners shudder at the thought of putting their puppy in a cage, "I could never do that!" they say. "It would be like putting my children in jail!" A puppy is not a child, however, and he has different needs and instincts. Puppies like to curl up in small, dark places. That's why they like to sleep under the coffee table or under a chair.

Because your Sheltie puppy does have an instinct to keep his bed clean, being confined in the crate will help him develop more bowel and bladder control. When he is confined for gradually extended periods of time, he will hold his wastes to avoid soiling his bed. It is your responsibility to make sure he isn't left too long.

The crate will also be your Sheltie puppy's place of refuge. If he's tired, hurt, or sick, allow him to go back to his crate to sleep or hide. If he's overstimulated or excited, put him back in his crate to calm down.

Because the crate physically confines the puppy, it can also prevent some unwanted behaviors such as destructive chewing or raiding the trash cans. When you cannot supervise the puppy or when you leave the house, put him in his crate and he will be prevented from getting into trouble.

Introducing the Crate

Introduce your puppy to the crate by propping open the door and tossing a treat inside. As you do this, tell your puppy, "Go to bed!" Let him go inside to get the treat. Let him investigate the crate and come and go as he wishes. When he's comfortable with that, offer him his next meal in the crate. Once he's in, close the door

Your Sheltie puppy will be happy to explore his new crate, especially when treats are involved.

Photo by Isabelle Francais

shetland sheepdog

behind him. Let him out when he's through eating. Offer several meals in the same fashion to show your puppy that the crate is a pretty neat place.

After your Sheltie puppy is used to going in and out for treats and meals, start feeding him back in his normal place again and go back to offering a treat for going into the crate. Tell him, "Sweetie, go to bed," and then give him his treat.

Don't let your puppy out of the crate during a temper tantrum. If he starts crying, screaming, throwing himself at the door, or scratching at the door, correct him verbally, "No, quiet!" or simply close the door to the room and walk away. If you let him out because he throws a tantrum, you will simply teach him that temper tantrums work. Instead, let him out when you are ready to let him out and when he is quiet.

Crate Location

The ideal place for the crate is in your bedroom, within arm's reach of the bed. This will give your Sheltie eight uninterrupted hours with you while you do nothing but sleep. In these busy times, that is quality time.

Having you nearby will give your Sheltie puppy a feeling of security, whereas exiling him to the laundry room or backyard will isolate him. He will be more apt to cry, whine, chew destructively, or get into other trouble because of loneliness and fear.

Having the crate close at night will save you some wear and tear, too. If he needs to go outside during the night (and he may need to for a few weeks) you will hear him whine, and you can let him out before he has an accident. If he's restless or bored, you can rap on the top of his crate and tell him to be quiet without getting out of bed.

HOUSEHOLD RULES

As has been mentioned before, it's important to start teaching your Sheltie puppy the household rules you wish him to observe as soon as possible. Your eight- to ten-week-old puppy is not too young to learn, and by starting early, you can prevent him from learning bad habits.

When deciding which rules you want him to learn, look at your Sheltie puppy not as the baby he is now but as the adult he will grow up to be. Are you going to want him up on the furniture when he's all grown up? Will you be bothered by dog hair on the sofa? Do you want him to jump up on people? Given their own way, all Shelties jump up, that's just the way they are. Do you want him to do that to the neighbor's children or to your grandmother?

Some rules you may want to institute could include teaching your Sheltie that jumping on people is not allowed, that he must behave when guests come to the house, that he should stay out of the kitchen, that he should leave the trash cans alone, and that he should chew only on his toys.

Teaching your Sheltie puppy these rules is not difficult. Be very clear with your corrections. When he does something wrong, correct him with a deep, firm tone of voice, "No jump!" When he does something right, use a higher pitched tone of voice, "Good boy to chew on your toy!" You must be very clear—either something is right or it is wrong, there are no shades of gray in between.

ACCEPTING THE LEASH

Learning to accept the leash can be difficult for some puppies. If your Sheltie learns to dislike the leash as a young puppy, he may continue to

A retractable leash is a practical choice for your Sheltie. They provide freedom for dogs while allowing the owner complete control. Leashes are available in a wide variety of lengths for all breeds. Photo courtesy of Flexi-USA, Inc.

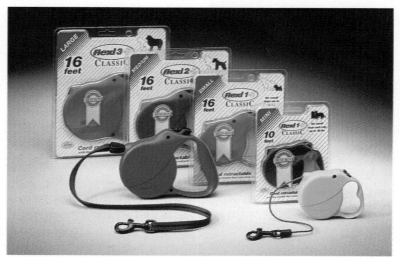

shetland sheepdog

resent it for many years. However, if he learns the leash is a key to more exciting things, he will welcome it.

Soon after you bring your puppy home, put a soft, buckle collar on his neck. Make sure it's loose enough to come over his head if he gets tangled up in something. Give him a day or two to get used to the collar. Then, when you are going to be close by and can supervise him, snap the leash onto the collar and let him drag it behind him. As he walks around, he will step on the leash, feel it tug on his

Learning to accept the leash can be difficult for puppies, so take it slowly and praise your Sheltie frequently.

Photo by Isabelle Francais

> **IF YOUR PUPPY BALKS**
>
> If your puppy balks, do not use the leash to drag him to you. This will cause him to dig his feet in and apply the brakes. Instead, kneel down, open your arms wide, and encourage him to come to you, "Hey, Sweetie, here! Good boy!" When he dashes to your lap, praise him and tell him what a wonderful puppy he is. Then try the exercise again.

neck, and in doing so, will get used to the feel of it.

After two or three short sessions like this, you can then teach your puppy to follow you on the leash. Have a few pieces of a soft, easily chewed treat that your puppy enjoys. Hold the leash in one hand and the treats in another. Show him the treat and back away a few steps as you tell your puppy, "Let's go! Good boy!" When he follows you a few steps, praise him and give him the treat. Sheltie puppies are usually easily motivated by food, and when he learns a treat is being offered, he should follow you with no problem.

Repeat two or three times and then stop the training session. Reward your puppy by giving him a tummy rub or by throwing the ball a few times.

After two or three training

session like this, make it more challenging by backing up slowly, quickly, or by making turns. If he gets confused or balks, make it simple again until he's willingly following you.

INTRODUCING THE CAR

Many puppies are afraid of the car because a ride in the car was the first strange thing to happen to them when they were taken from their mother and littermates. The car also takes them to the veterinarian's

END ON A HIGH NOTE
Always end these (and all) training sessions on a high note. If your Sheltie puppy is worried, scared, or confused, help him do something right and then end the training session with that praise. Never end the training session at a negative point in the training, or that will affect his outlook toward training later.

office, another strange place where someone in a white coat pokes them, prods them, and gives them shots. You don't want this fear of the car to grab hold, though—you want your puppy to understand that riding in the car is something fun to do.

Start by lifting your puppy into the car and handing him a treat. As soon as he finishes the treat, lift him down and walk away. Repeat this simple exercise several times a day for a few days. Then lift him into the car, give him a treat, let him eat it, and let him explore the car for a few minutes. After he has sniffed for a few minutes, give him another treat, let him eat it, then lift him down and walk away. Continue this training for a week or two, depending on how nervous your puppy is in the car.

When your puppy is

Once your puppy has learned to love car rides, using a crate or specially designed doggie seatbelt is the best way to keep your road trips safe.

Photo by Isabelle Francais

expecting a treat in the car, put his crate in the car and strap it down securely. Put your puppy in his crate, give him a treat, and then start the car's engine. Back down the driveway and return to the house. Stop the engine, give your puppy a treat, and let him out of his crate and the car.

The next time, drive down the street and back. Then go around the block. Increase the distances and times of the drives very gradually. Keep in mind, you want your puppy to expect good things in the car, not scary things. Your Sheltie puppy will have a lifetime of car rides ahead of him, and life will be much nicer if he enjoys the rides.

SOCIAL HANDLING

Your Sheltie puppy cannot care for himself. You must be able to brush and comb him, bathe him, check his feet for cuts and scrapes, and clean his ears. Your Sheltie puppy doesn't understand why you need to do these annoying things to him, and he may struggle when you try to care for him. This social handling exercise will help teach your puppy to accept your care.

Sit down on the floor with your puppy and have him lie down between your legs. He can lie on his back or his side; let him get comfortable. Start by giving him a slow, easy tummy rub. The idea here is to relax him. If your movements are fast and vigorous, you'll make him want to play, so keep it slow and gentle. If he starts to struggle, tell him calmly, "Easy. Be still." Restrain him gently if you need to do so.

When your puppy is relaxed, start giving him a massage. Start at his neck and ears, gently rubbing all around the base of

Start your puppy's massage at his neck and ears, and work your way down. He will soon relax and learn to enjoy the attention.

Photo by Isabelle Francais

shetland sheepdog

Even a small puppy must get used to handling and grooming, so don't let cumbersome grooming tools stop you from getting the job done. There are compact, lightweight tools available. Photo courtesy of Wahl, USA.

RELAX!

You can also use the social handling exercise to relax your puppy when he's overstimulated. If you let him in from the backyard and he's full of Sheltie energy, don't chase him down or try to correct him. Instead, sit down on the floor and invite him to join you. (Use a treat to get him to come to you if you need some extra incentive.) Once he's come to you, lay him down and begin the massage. He will relax and calm down and in the process, you are also giving him the attention he needs from you.

All training sessions should end happily. Help your dog do something correctly, then praise him and give him a treat.

each ear and working down the neck to the shoulders. Continue over his body, gently massaging it while at the same time you check his body for cuts, scratches, lumps, bumps, bruises, fleas, ticks, or any other problems that need to be taken care of.

Once your puppy has learned to enjoy this handling, you can clean his ears, wash out his eyes, trim his toenails, or do anything else that needs doing during the massage.

Photo by Isabelle Francais

shetland sheepdog

The Basic
OBEDIENCE
Commands

Many dog owners don't admit their dog needs training. "He does everything I ask," they say. Yet when asked specific questions about behavior, the answer changes. A trained Sheltie won't jump up on people, dash out the open door, or herd the family cat.

Dog owners benefit from training, too. During training, you learn how to teach your Sheltie and how to motivate him so that he wants to be good. You also learn how to prevent problem behavior from happening and how to correct mistakes that do happen.

THE TEACHING PROCESS

Although Shelties are a very intelligent breed with a long history of working for people, you cannot simply tell your Sheltie to do something and expect him to understand your verbal language. Training is a process that begins with teaching your dog that certain words have meanings and that you would like him to follow your directions. Your Sheltie, however, doesn't understand

THE IMPORTANCE OF TRAINING

When you decided to add a Shetland Sheepdog to your family, you probably did so because you wanted a companion, a friend, a protector, and a confidant. You may have wanted a dog to go for walks with you, run along the beach, catch tennis balls, and hike in the mountains. You may have wanted your children to have the same relationship with a dog that you remember from your childhood. To do any of these things, your Sheltie will need training.

why you want him to do these things—after all, why should he sit? He doesn't know why sitting is so important to you. Therefore, training is a process.

Show Your Dog

First of all, you want to show your dog what it is you want him to do and that there is a word—a human spoken sound—associated with that action or position. For example, when teaching him to sit, you can help him into position as you tell him, "Sweetie, sit." Follow that with praise, "Good boy to sit!" Praise him even if you

Photo by Isabelle Francais

Good training helps strengthen the loving relationship between dog and owner.

Shelties are very intelligent dogs and will quickly figure this out. Instead, give enthusiastic praise when he makes an effort and does something right for you.

Correct

Do not correct your dog until he understands what it is you want him to do. After he understands, is willing to obey the command, and then chooses *not* to do it, you can correct him with a verbal correction, "Sweetie, no!" or a quick snap and release of the collar. Use *only* as much correction as is needed to get

helped him into position.

You will follow a similar pattern when teaching your dog most new things. If you want him off the sofa, you can tell him, "Sweetie, off the furniture," as you take him by the collar and pull him off. When he gets down, tell him, "Good boy to get off the furniture."

Praise

Praise him every time he does something right, even if you help him do it. Your Sheltie will pay more attention and try harder if he is praised for his efforts. However, don't praise him when it's undeserved.

USE INTERRUPTIONS

Interrupt incorrect behavior as you see it happen. If your dog is walking by the kitchen trash can and turns to sniff it, interrupt him, "Leave it alone!" If you tell him to sit and he does sit, but then starts to get up, interrupt him, "No! Sit." By interrupting him, you can stop incorrect behavior before or as it happens. Interruptions and corrections alone will not teach your Sheltie; they are used to stop undesirable behavior or actions at that precise moment. Your Sheltie learns much more when you reward good behavior. Stop the behavior you don't want, but lavishly praise the actions you want to continue.

his attention and *no more*. With corrections, less is usually better as long as your dog is responding.

Your Timing

The timing of your praise, corrections, and interruptions is very important. Praise him *as* he is doing something right. Correct him *when* he makes the mistake. Interrupt him *as* he starts to stick his nose into the trash can. If your timing is slow, he may not understand what you are trying to teach him.

Be Fair

Shelties resent corrections that are too harsh or unfair. They will show this resentment by refusing to work, planting themselves and refusing to move, or fighting back. Some Shelties will even show signs of depression if a harsh training method continues.

THE BASIC COMMANDS

Sit and Release

The sit is the foundation command for everything else your Sheltie will learn. When your Sheltie learns to sit and sit still, he learns to control himself and that there are consequences to his actions.

This is a very big lesson.

The sit is also a good alternative action for problem behavior. Your Sheltie cannot both sit still and jump on you. Learning to sit still for praise can replace jumping up on people for attention. He can't knock his food bowl out of your hand if he's sitting still, waiting patiently for his dinner. You can fasten his leash to his collar more easily if he's sitting still. This is a practical, useful command!

There are two basic methods of teaching your Sheltie to sit. Some dogs do better using one technique than the other, so try both and see which is better for your Sheltie.

Hold your Sheltie's leash in your left hand and have some treats in your right hand. Tell your Sheltie, "Sweetie, sit!" as you move your right hand (with the treats) from his nose over his head toward his tail. He will lift his head to watch your hand. As his head goes up and back, his hips will go down. As he sits, praise him, "Good boy to sit!" and give him a treat. Pet him in the sitting position.

When you are ready for him to get up, tap him on the shoulder as you tell him, "Release!" Each exercise needs a beginning and an end. The sit command is the beginning, and the release command tells him he is done and can move now. If he doesn't get up on his own, use your hands on his collar to walk him forward.

If your Sheltie is too excited by the treats to think (and some Shelties are like that), put the treats away. Tell your Sheltie to sit as you place one hand under his chin on the front of the neck as you slide the other hand down his hips to tuck under his back legs. Gently shape him into a sit as you give him the command, "Sweetie, sit." Praise him and release him.

If your dog is wiggly as you try and teach this exercise, keep your hands on him. If he pops up, interrupt that action with a deep, firm tone of voice, "Be still!" When he responds and

> **ONE COMMAND**
> Don't keep repeating any command. The command is not, "Sit! Sit, sit, sit, please sit. SIT!!" If you give repeated commands for the sit, your Sheltie will assume that carries over to everything else. Tell him one time to sit and then help him do it.

stops wiggling, praise him quietly and gently.

Down

The down exercise continues one of the lessons the sit command started, that of self-control. It is hard for many energetic, bouncy young Shelties to control their own actions, but it is a lesson all must learn. Practicing the down exercise teaches your Sheltie to lie down and be still.

You can teach your Sheltie to sit by holding a treat and motioning your hand over his head toward his tail. If that doesn't work, shape his hind legs into the sit position as you give the command.

Photo by Isabelle Francais

For the down exercise, start with your Sheltie in the sit position. Then take a treat straight down to the ground in front of him as you give the command.

SIT, PLEASE!

Once your Sheltie understands the sit command, start having him sit for everything he wants. Have him sit before you give him a treat, before you let him have his meals, and before you pet him. When he comes up to you and nudges your arm, asking you to pet him, have him sit before you pet him. Shelties have a long working history, but as a housepet, they have no job. Give your Sheltie a job to do—his first one is to sit for everything he wants!

Start with your Sheltie in a sit. Rest one hand gently on his shoulder and have a treat in the other hand. Let him smell the treat and then tell him, "Sweetie, down" and take the treat straight down to the ground in front of his front paws. As he follows the treat down, use your hand on his shoulders to encourage him to lie down. Praise him, give him the treat, and then have him hold the position for a moment. Then release him in the same way you did from the sit; pat him on the shoulder, tell him "Release!" and let him get up.

If your dog looks at the treat as you make the signal but doesn't follow the treat to the

If your Sheltie learns that he has to sit when you greet someone and before anyone can pet him, he won't jump on people.

ground, simply scoop his front legs up and forward as you lay him down. The rest of the exercise is the same.

As your Sheltie learns what the down command means, you can have him hold it for a few minutes longer before you release him, but do not step away from him yet. Stay next to him, and if he's wiggly, keep a hand on his shoulder to help him stay in position.

Stay

When your Sheltie understands both the sit and down commands, you can introduce him to the stay exercise. You want to convey to your Sheltie that the word "stay" means "hold still." When your dog is sitting and you tell

> ### LIE DOWN FOR A TUMMY RUB
>
> You don't want the down command to be looked at as a negative exercise or as punishment, so at least once every day have your Sheltie lie down and once he's down, roll him over and give him a nice relaxing tummy rub. When he's happy and definitely enjoying his training, release him from the down and tell him what a wonderful dog he is.

him to stay, you want him to remain in the sitting position until you go back to him and release him. When you tell him to stay while he's lying down, you want him to remain lying down until you go back to him to release him from that position. Eventually, he will be

If your Sheltie is wiggly and uncooperative, gently hold him in the down position until you are ready to release him.

shetland sheepdog

able to hold the sit position for several minutes and the down for even longer.

Start by having your Sheltie sit. With the leash in your left hand, use the leash to put a slight bit of pressure backward (toward his tail) as you tell him, "Sweetie, stay." At the same time, use your right hand to give your dog a hand signal that will mean stay—an open-handed gesture with the palm toward your dog's face. Take one step away and, at the same time, release the pressure on the leash.

If your dog moves or gets up, tell him "No!" so that he knows he made a mistake and put him back into position. Repeat the exercise. After a few seconds, go back to him and praise him. Don't let him move from position until you release him. Use the same process to teach

> **BE CLEAR**
> Make sure you are very clear to your dog what you want him to do. Remember, something is either right or wrong to your dog. It's not partly right or partly wrong. Be fair with your commands, your praise, and your corrections.

the stay in the down position.

With the stay commands, you always want to go back to your Sheltie to release him. Don't release him from a distance or call him to come to you from the stay. If you do either of these, your dog will be much less reliable on the stay; he will continue to get up from the stay because you will have taught him to do exactly that. When teaching the stay, you want your Sheltie to learn that stay means "Hold this position until I come back to you to

To teach the down/stay, have your Sheltie go into the down position. Use an open-handed gesture toward the dog's face, and back away slowly.

release you."

As your Sheltie learns the stay command, you can gradually increase the time you ask him to hold it. However, if your dog is making a lot of mistakes and moving often, you are either asking your dog to hold it too long or your dog doesn't understand the command yet. In either case, go back and reteach the exercise from the beginning.

Increase the distance from your dog very gradually, too. Again, if your dog is making a lot of mistakes, you're moving away too quickly. Teach everything very gradually.

When your Sheltie understands the stay command but chooses not to do it, you need to let him know the command is not optional. Many young, wiggly Shelties want to

A well-trained Sheltie knows that "stay" means that he should do just that.

Photo by Isabelle Francais

USING THE STAY COMMAND

You can use the stay command around the house. For example, in the evening while you're watching a favorite television show, have your Sheltie lie down at your feet while you sit on the sofa. Give him a toy to chew on and tell him, "Sweetie, stay." Have him do a down/stay when your guests visit so he isn't jumping all over them. Have him lie down and stay while the family is eating so he isn't begging under the table. There are a lot of practical uses for the stay—just look at your normal routine and see where this command can work for you.

do anything *except* hold still, but holding still is very important to Sheltie owners! Correct excess movement first with your voice: "No! Be still! Stay!" and if that doesn't stop the excess movement, use a verbal correction and a snap and release of the leash. When he does control himself, praise him enthusiastically, but not so enthusiastically that he moves again.

Watch Me

The watch me exercise teaches your Sheltie to ignore distractions and pay attention to you. This is particularly useful when you're out in public and your dog is distracted by children playing or dogs barking behind a fence.

Start by having your Sheltie sit in front of you. Have a treat in your right hand. Let him sniff the treat, and then tell him, "Sweetie, watch me!" as you take the treat from his nose up to your chin. When his eyes follow the treat in your hand and he looks at your face, praise him, "Good boy to watch me!" and give him the treat. Then release him from the sit. Repeat it again exactly the same way two or three times, and then stop the training session.

The stay command is very useful around the house. This Sheltie has learned to stay in the kitchen while his family eats in the dining room.

If your Sheltie likes to pull you along when he's on a leash, try a no-pull training halter that's guaranteed by the manufacturer to stop any dog from pulling. Photo courtesy of Four Paws.

Because this is hard for young, bouncing Shelties, practice it first at home when there are few distractions. However, once he knows it well inside, then you must try it with distractions. Take him out in the front yard (on his leash, of course) and tell him to watch you. If he ignores you, take his chin in your left hand (with the treat in the right) and hold it so that he has to look at your face. Praise him even though you are helping him do it.

When he will watch you outside where there are

Photo by Isabelle Francais

Photo by Isabelle Francais

The watch me exercise trains your dog to ignore outdoor distractions and focus on you.

shetland sheepdog

distractions, then move on to the next step. Have him sit in front of you and tell him to watch you. As he watches you, take a few steps backward and ask him to follow you and watch you at the same time. Praise him when he does. Try it again. When he can follow you six or seven steps and watch you at the same time, make it more challenging—back up and turn to the left or right, or back up faster. Praise him when he continues to watch you.

Heel

You want your Sheltie to learn that heel means "Walk by my left side, with your neck and shoulders by my left leg, and maintain that position." Ideally, your Sheltie should maintain that position as you walk slowly, quickly, turn corners, or weave in and out through a crowd.

To start, practice a "Watch me" exercise to get your dog's attention. Back away from him and encourage him to watch you. When he does, simply turn your body as you are backing up so that your dog ends up on your left side, and continue walking. If you have done it correctly, it is one smooth movement so you and your dog end up walking forward together with your dog on your left side.

Let's walk it through in slow motion. Sit your dog in front of you and do a "Watch me." Back away from your dog, and encourage him to follow you. When he's watching you, back up toward your left and as you are backing, continue turning in that direction so you and your

When teaching your dog to heel, begin by backing up with a treat in hand and coaxing him to follow you. Then, smoothly turn so you are walking next to him.

dog end up walking forward together. Your dog should end up on your left side (or you should end up on your dog's right side).

If your dog starts to pull forward, simply back away from him and encourage him to follow you. If you need to do so, use the leash with a snap-and-release motion to make the dog follow you. Praise him when he does.

Don't hesitate to go back and forth—walking forward and then backing away—if you need to do so. In fact, sometimes this can be the best exercise you can do to get your dog's attention on you.

When your dog is walking nicely with you and paying attention to you, then you can

> **DON'T USE THE COME COMMAND TO PUNISH**
> Never call your Sheltie to come to you and then punish him for something he did earlier. Not only is late punishment ineffective (it never works!) but that unfair punishment will teach your Sheltie to avoid you when you call him. Is that what you want him to learn? Keep the come command positive.

start eliminating the backing away. Start the heel with your Sheltie sitting by your left side. Tell him, "Sweetie, watch me! Heel." Start walking. When he's walking nicely with you, praise him. However, if he gets distracted or starts to pull, simply back away from him again.

Come

The come command is one of the most important commands your Sheltie needs to learn. Not only is the come command important around the house in your daily routine, but it could also be a lifesaver some day, especially if he should decide to dash toward the street when a car is coming. Because the come command is so important, you will use two different techniques to teach your dog to come to you when you call him.

Once your Sheltie has learned to heel, walks will be much more fun for both of you.

Photo by Isabelle Francais

shetland sheepdog

Come with a Treat

The first technique will use a sound stimulus and a treat to teach your Sheltie to come when you call him. Take a small plastic container (such as a margarine tub) and put a handful of dry dog food in it. Put the lid on and shake it. It should make a nice rattling sound.

Have the shaker in one hand and some good dog treats in the other. Shake the container, and as your Sheltie looks at it and you, ask him, "Sweetie, cookie?" Use whatever word he already knows means treat. When you say "cookie," pop a treat in his mouth. Do it again. Shake, shake, say "Sweetie, cookie?" and pop a treat in his mouth.

The sound of the container, your verbal question, and the treat are all becoming associated in his mind. He is learning that the sound of the container equals the treat—an important lesson! Do this several times a day for several days.

Then, with him sitting in front of you, replace the word "cookie" with the word "come." Shake the container, say "Sweetie, come!" and pop a treat in his mouth. You are rewarding him even though he

USING A SOUND STIMULUS

Do you remember those silent dog whistles that used to be advertised in comic books? There was nothing magical about those whistles, except that they were so high-pitched, dogs could hear them but people couldn't. The container we're using to teach the come command works on the same principle that the silent dog whistle used—it's a sound stimulus you can use to get the dog's attention so that you can teach him. By teaching him to pay attention to the sound of the shaker, and by teaching him that the sound of the shaker means he's going to get a treat, we can make coming when called that much more exciting. Your dog will be more likely to come to you (especially when there are distractions) if he's excited about it.

didn't actually come to you—he was already sitting in front of you. However, you are teaching him that the sound of the shaker now equals the word "come," and he still gets the treat. Another important lesson. Practice this several times a day for several days.

When your Sheltie is happy to hear the shaker and is drooling to get a treat, start calling him across the room. Shake the container as you say, "Sweetie, come!" When he

Teaching your dog to come when you call him by using a shaker and treats is well worth the effort.

dashes to you, continue to give him a treat as you praise him, "Good boy to come!" Practice this up and down the hallway, inside and outside, and across the backyard. Make it fun, keeping up with the treats and the verbal praise.

Come with a Long Line

The second method to teach your dog to come uses a long leash or a length of clothesline rope. Because Shelties are athletic and fast, have a line at least 30 feet in length. Fasten the line to your Sheltie's collar, and then let him go play. When he is distracted by something, call him with, "Sweetie, come!" If he responds and comes right away, praise him.

If he doesn't respond right away, do *not* call him again. Pick up the line, back away from

DON'T WORRY

Some people have reservations about this technique because they are worried the dog will not come to them when they don't have a treat. First of all, you will use two different techniques to teach the come and only one technique uses the treats. Second, even with the first technique, you will eventually stop using treats. However, by using this technique when first introducing the come command, you can produce such a strong, reliable response, it's worth all of your efforts.

him, and using the line, *make* him come to you. Do not give him a verbal correction at this time; he may associate the verbal correction with coming to you. Instead, simply make him come to you even if you have to drag him in with the

Treats are a great way to motivate your Sheltie to learn. Once he knows the basic obedience commands, you can wean him from the treats.

Photo by Isabelle Francais

shetland sheepdog

Teaching the come command with the Sheltie on a long line gives you control if your dog is distracted.

shetland sheepdog

NEVER END PLAYTIME WITH THE COME COMMAND

When you let your Sheltie run and play, do you call him to come when you end the play session? Many dog owners do, and that quickly teaches your dog that the come command means the end of all the fun. In response, the dog refuses to come and this refusal becomes a permanent problem. Instead of calling your dog to come only at the end of the play sessions, incorporate it into the sessions. Call your dog in a very happy tone of voice, run away from him as you call him so that he wants to chase you, and then praise him when he catches you. Then—and this is the important part—give him permission to go play again! Do this several times throughout his playtime, each time rewarding him for coming with praise, play, or a treat, and then giving him permission to continue his play. Your Sheltie will think the come command is just as exciting as the play.

USE IT OR LOSE IT

The best way to make this training work for you and your Sheltie is to use it. Training is not just for training sessions—instead, training is for your daily life. Incorporate it into your daily routine. Have your Sheltie sit before you feed him. Have him lie down and stay while you eat. Have him sit and stay at the gate while you take the trash cans out. Have him do a down/stay when guests come over. Use these commands as part of your life. They will work much better that way.

treats help keep his attention, use them. However, eventually you will want him to be able to practice the come on the long line without the treats or the sound of the shaker.

Don't allow your Sheltie to have freedom off the leash until he is grown up enough to handle the responsibility and is very well trained. Many dog owners let their dog off leash much too soon, and the dogs learn bad habits their owners wish they hadn't learned. Each time your dog learns that he can ignore you or run away from you, it reinforces the fact that he can. Instead, let him run around and play while dragging the long line. That way you can always regain control when you need it.

line. Let him go again and repeat the entire exercise. Make sure you always praise him when he does decide to come to you.

If he is very distracted, use the shaker and treats along with the long line—remember, we want him to be able to succeed in his training. If the shaker and

All About
FORMAL 5
Training

Formal dog training is much more than the traditional sit, down, stay, and come commands. It means teaching your Sheltie that he's living in your house, not his. It means you can set some rules and expect him to follow them. It will not turn your Sheltie into a robot—instead, it will teach your Sheltie to look at you in a new light. Training will cause you to look at him differently, too. Training is not something you do *to* your Sheltie, it's something you do together.

TRAINING METHODS

If you were to talk to 100 dog trainers (someone who trains dogs) or dog obedience instructors (someone who teaches the dog owner how to teach his dog) and ask them how they train, you would get 100 different answers. Any trainer or instructor who has been in the business for any

Formal training might prepare you and your dog for conformation or obedience competitions.

shetland sheepdog

period of time is going to work out a method or technique that works best for her. Each method will be based on the trainer's personality, teaching techniques, experience, and philosophy regarding dogs and dog training. Any given method may work wonderfully for one trainer but fail terribly for another.

Because there are so many different techniques, styles, and methods, choosing a particular instructor may be difficult. It is important to understand some of the different methods so that you can make a reasonable decision.

Compulsive Training

Compulsive training is a method of training that forces the dog to behave. This is usually a correction-based training style, sometimes with forceful corrections. This training is usually used with law enforcement and military dogs and can be quite effective with hard-driving, strong-willed dogs. Many pet dog owners do not like this style of training, feeling it is too rough.

This type of training is too forceful for most Shelties. Although Shetland Sheepdogs can be tough herding dogs, their relationship with their owner can be much more sensitive. A harsh training method could cause the Sheltie to withdraw or even become despondent.

Inducive Training

This training is exactly the opposite of compulsive training. Instead of being forced to do something, the dog is induced or motivated toward proper behavior. Depending on the instructor, there are few or no corrections used. This training works very well for most puppies, for softer dogs, and sometimes for owners who dislike corrections of any kind.

Unfortunately, this is not the right technique for all Shelties.

An inducive training style motivates a dog toward appropriate behavior using rewards but few or no corrections.

Photo by Isabelle Francais

Many Shelties will take advantage of the lack of corrections or discipline. Some very intelligent dogs with very dominant personalities (including some Shelties) look upon the lack of discipline as weakness on your part and will then set their own rules which, unfortunately, may not be the rules you wish to have.

Somewhere in the Middle

The majority of trainers and instructors use a training method that is somewhere in between both of these techniques. An inducive method is used when possible, while corrections are used when needed. Obviously the range can be vast, with some trainers leaning toward more corrections, and others using as few as possible. A training program such as this is usually the most successful for Shelties.

GROUP CLASSES OR PRIVATE LESSONS?

There are benefits and drawbacks to both group classes and private lessons. In group classes, the dog must learn to behave around other distractions, specifically the other dogs and people in class. Because the world is made up of lots of things capable of distracting your Sheltie, this can work very well. In addition, a

A group dog training class will teach your Sheltie to behave even when other people and dogs are present.

shetland sheepdog

group class can work like group therapy for dog owners. The owners can share triumphs and mishaps and can encourage and support one another. Many friendships have begun in group training classes.

The drawback to group classes is that for some dogs, the distractions of a group class are too much. Some dogs simply cannot concentrate at all, especially in the beginning of training. For these dogs, a few private lessons may help enough so that the dog can join a group class later. Dogs with severe behavior problems—especially aggression—should bypass group classes for obvious reasons.

Private lessons—one-on-one training with the owner, dog, and instructor—are also good for people with a very busy schedule who may otherwise not be able to do any training at all.

Puppy Class

Puppy or kindergarten classes are for puppies over 10 weeks of age but not over 16 weeks. These classes are usually half obedience training and half socialization, because for puppies, both of these subjects are very important. The puppy's owner also learns how to

prevent problem behaviors from occurring and how to establish household rules.

Basic Obedience Class

This class is for puppies that have graduated from a puppy class, for puppies more than four months of age that haven't attended a puppy class, or for adult dogs. In this class, the dogs and their owners work on basic obedience commands such as sit, down, stay, come, and heel. Most instructors also spend time discussing problem prevention and problem solving, especially the common problems like jumping on people, barking, digging, and chewing.

Dog Sports Training

Some instructors offer training for one or more of the various dog activities or sports. There are classes to prepare you for competition in

ADVANCED TRAINING
Advanced training classes vary depending on the instructor. Some offer classes to teach you to control your dog off leash, some emphasize dog sports, and others may simply continue basic training skills. Ask the instructor what she offers.

obedience trials, conformation dog shows, flyball, agility, or herding. Other trainers may offer training for noncompetitive activities such as therapy dog work.

FINDING AN INSTRUCTOR OR TRAINER

When trying to find an instructor or trainer, word-of-mouth referrals are probably the best place to start. Anyone can place an advertisement in the newspaper or yellow pages—the ad itself is no guarantee of quality or expertise. However, happy customers will demonstrate their experience with well-behaved dogs and will be glad

GOALS FOR YOUR SHELTIE

What do you want training to accomplish? Do you want your Sheltie to be calm and well-behaved around family members? Do you want him to behave himself out in public? Would you like to participate in dog activities and sports? There are an unlimited number of things you can do with your Sheltie—it's up to you to decide what you would like to do. Then you can find a training program to help you achieve those goals. As you start training, talk to your trainer about them so she can guide you in the right direction.

to tell you where they received instruction.

Have you admired a

Improve your puppy's social skills by signing him up for puppy classes and exposing him to new people and other animals.

Photo by Judith E. Strom

s h e t l a n d   s h e e p d o g

Photo by Isabelle Francais

When looking for a good dog trainer, get recommendations from other dog owners. For example, find out where your neighbor's well-behaved dogs received instruction.

shetland sheepdog

neighbor's well-behaved dog? Ask where they went for training. Call your veterinarian, local pet store, or groomer, and ask who they recommend. Make notes about each referral. What did people like about this trainer? What did they dislike?

Once you have a list of referrals, start calling the instructors and ask a few questions. How long has she been teaching classes? You will want someone with experience, of course, so that she can handle the various situations that may arise. However, experience is not the only qualification. Some people that have been training for years are still teaching exactly the same way they did many years ago and have never learned anything new.

Ask the instructor about Shelties. What does she think of the breed? Ideally, she should be knowledgeable about the breed, what makes them tick, and how to train them. If she doesn't like the breed, go elsewhere.

Ask the instructor to explain her training methods. Does this sound like something you would be comfortable with? Ask if there are alternative methods used. Not every dog will respond the same way, and every instructor should have a backup plan.

Does the instructor belong to any professional organizations? The National Association of Dog Obedience Instructors (NADOI) and the Association of Pet Dog Trainers (APDT) are two of the more prominent groups. Both of these organizations publish regular newsletters to share information, techniques, new developments, and more. Instructors belonging to organizations such as these are more likely to be up-to-date on training techniques, styles, and so forth, as well as information about specific dog breeds.

Make sure, too, that the instructor will be able to help you achieve your goals. For example, if you want to compete in obedience trials, the instructor should have experience in that field and knowledge of the rules and regulations concerning that competition.

After talking to several trainers or instructors, ask if you can watch their training sessions or classes. If they say no, cross them off your list. There should be no reason why you cannot attend one class to see if you will be comfortable with an instructor and her style of teaching. As you watch the class, see how she handles students' dogs. Would you let her handle your dog? How does she relate to the students? Are they relaxed? Do they look like they're having a good time? Are they paying attention to her?

After talking to the instructor or trainer and after watching a class, you should be able to make a decision as to what class you want to attend. If you're still undecided, call the instructor back and ask a few more questions. After all, you are hiring her to provide a service, and you must be comfortable with your decision.

BUILDING A RELATIONSHIP

Training helps build a relationship between you and your dog. This relationship is built on mutual trust, affection, and respect. Training can help your dog become your best friend; a well-behaved companion that is a joy to spend time with and one that won't send your blood pressure sky-high.

Both you and your Sheltie must be comfortable with your trainer's technique.

Photo by Isabelle Francais

shetland sheepdog

Problem
PREVENTION
and Solving

Shelties are an intelligent breed that loves to be active. That activity level can, unfortunately, get the dogs into trouble. Because Shelties are also easily trained, many Sheltie owners are flabbergasted when they find their beloved dog has chewed up the sofa cushion or chased the family cat to the top of the china hutch. Unfortunately, problem behavior can have many causes, and solving it isn't always easy.

Many of the behaviors that dog owners consider

> ### TRAINING
> Training can play a big part in controlling problem behavior. A fair, upbeat, yet firm training program teaches your dog that you are in charge and that he is below you in the family pack. Training should also reinforce his concept of you as a kind, calm, caring leader. In addition, your training skills give you the ability to teach your dog what is acceptable and what is not.

problems—barking, digging, chewing, jumping up on people, and so on—aren't problems to your Sheltie. In fact, they are

Shelties need to be active. Their high energy level can sometimes cause problem behavior.

Photo by Isabelle Francais

s h e t l a n d   s h e e p d o g

Proper nutrition is imperative to your dog's health. Veterinarians recommend elevated feeders to help reduce stress on your dog's neck and back muscles. The raised platform also provides better digestion while reducing bloating and gas. Photo courtesy of Pet Zone Products, Ltd.

very natural behaviors to your Sheltie. Shelties like to jump up on people. Dogs dig because the dirt smells good or because there's a gopher in the yard. Dogs bark to verbalize something, just as people talk. However, most problem behavior can be addressed and either prevented, controlled, or in some cases, stopped entirely.

WHAT YOU CAN DO

Health Problems

Some experts think that 20 percent of all behavior problems commonly seen are caused by health problems. A bladder infection or a gastrointestinal upset

commonly causes housetraining accidents. Thyroid problems can cause a behavior change, as can medications, hyperactivity, hormone imbalances, and a variety of other health problems.

If your dog's behavior changes, make an appointment with your veterinarian. Tell your vet why you are bringing the dog in—don't just ask for an exam. Explain that your Sheltie has changed his behavior, tell the vet what the behavior is, and ask if he could do an exam for any physical problems that could lead to that type of behavior.

Don't automatically assume your dog is healthy. If a health

problem is causing the behavior change, training or behavior modification won't make it better. Before beginning any training, talk to your veterinarian. Once health problems are ruled out, then you can start working on the problem.

Nutrition

Nutrition can play a part in causing or solving behavior problems. If your dog is eating a poor-quality food, or if he cannot digest the food he is being fed, his body may be missing some vital nutrients. If your Sheltie is chewing on rocks or wood, chewing the stucco off the side of your house, or grazing on the plants in your garden, he may have a nutritional deficiency of some kind.

Some dogs develop a type of hyperactivity when fed a high-calorie, high-fat dog food. Other dogs have food allergies that may show up as behavior problems.

If you have any questions about the food your dog is eating, talk to your veterinarian.

Play

Play is different from exercise, although exercise can be play. The key to play is laughter. Researchers know that

Proper nutrition may help you solve behavior problems. The use of better ingredients in your dog's food leads to better nutrition and therefore to better health. Make sure the dog food you choose contains only the highest quality ingredients. Photo courtesy of Nutro Products, Inc.

shetland sheepdog

EXERCISE

Exercise is just as important for your Sheltie as it is for you. Exercise works the body, uses up excess energy, relieves stress, and clears the mind. How much exercise is needed depends on your dog and your normal routine. A fast-paced walk might be enough for an older Sheltie, but a young, healthy Sheltie might need a good run or game of fetch with a tennis ball.

Laughter and play have a special place in your relationship with your Sheltie. Shelties can be very silly, and you should take advantage of that. Laugh at him and with him. Play games that will make you laugh.

Play is also a great stress reliever. Make time for play when you are having a hard time at work. Play with your Sheltie after your training sessions.

Sometimes dogs get into trouble intentionally because they feel ignored. To these dogs, any attention—even corrections or yelling—is better than no attention at all. If you take time regularly to play with your dog, you can avoid some of these situations.

laughter is wonderful medicine. When you laugh, you feel better about the world around you.

Twenty percent of all behavior problems in dogs are health-related. Have your Sheltie examined by a vet if his behavior changes.

Prevent Problems From Happening

Because so many of the things we consider problems are natural behaviors to your Sheltie, you need to prevent as many of them from happening as you reasonably can. Put the trash cans away so that he never discovers that the kitchen trash can is full of good-tasting surprises. Make sure the kids put their toys away so that your Sheltie can't chew them to pieces. It's much easier to

Photo by Isabelle Francais

prevent a problem from happening than it is to break a bad habit later.

Preventing problems might require that you fence off the garden, build higher shelves in the garage, or maybe even build your Sheltie a dog run.

Part of preventing problems from occurring also requires that you limit your dog's freedom. A young puppy or untrained dog should never have unsupervised free run of the house; there is simply too much he can get into. Instead, keep him close to you and close off rooms. If you can't watch him, put him into his run or out in the backyard.

DEALING WITH SPECIFIC PROBLEMS

The Barker

Shelties are, unfortunately, often problem barkers. It is the breed's instinct to protect their territory, and anyone walking past the house is an intruder. In addition, a Sheltie left alone for many hours each day may find that barking gets him attention, especially if your neighbors yell at him.

Start teaching him to be quiet when you're at home with him. When your Sheltie starts barking, tell him, "Quiet!" When

A DOG RUN

A dog run is not a dog prison. Instead, it is a safe place for him where he can stay while he's unsupervised. In his dog run, he should have protection from the sun and weather, unspillable water, and a few toys. Don't put him in his run as punishment and never scold him in his run. Instead, give him a treat or a toy. Leave a radio playing quiet, gentle music in a nearby window.

he stops, praise him. When he understands what you want, go for a short walk outside, leaving him home. Listen, and when you

A good dog run will keep your Sheltie out of trouble. It should include protection from the weather, a solid fence, and a comfortable place to sleep.

Photo by Isabelle Francais

hear him start barking, come back and correct him. After a few corrections, when he seems to understand, ask a neighbor to help you. Go outside and ask your neighbor to come out to talk. Have the kids outside playing. When your dog barks because he's feeling left out, go back and correct him. Repeat as often as you need to until he understands.

You can reduce your dog's emotional need to bark if you make coming home and leaving home quiet and low-keyed. When you leave the house, don't give him hugs and don't

If your Sheltie is a problem barker, there are plenty of techniques that will teach him to be quiet.

Photo by Isabelle Francais

tell him repeatedly to be a good dog—that simply makes your leaving a more emotional event. Instead, give him attention an hour or two prior to your leaving, and when it's time for you to go, just go. When you come home, ignore your dog for a few minutes. Then whisper hello to him. Your Sheltie's hearing is very good, but to hear your whispers he is going to have to be quiet and still.

You can also distract your dog when you leave. Take a brown paper lunch bag and put a couple of treats in it; maybe a dog biscuit, a piece of carrot, and a slice of apple. Roll the top over to close it and rip a very tiny hole in the side to give your dog encouragement to get the treats. As you walk out the door or gate, hand this to your dog. He will be so busy figuring out where the treats are and how to get them, he'll forget you are leaving.

Jumping on People

Just about every Sheltie owner, at one time or another, has to deal with their dog jumping up on people. You can, however, control the jumping by emphasizing the sit. If your Sheltie is sitting, he can't jump up. By teaching him to sit for petting, praise, treats, and for his meals, you can teach him that the sit is important and that everything he wants will happen only when he sits.

Use the leash as much as you can to teach your Sheltie to sit. When you come home from work, don't greet your dog until you have a leash and collar in hand. As your dog greets you, slip the leash over his head. Then you can help him sit. If he tries to jump, give him a snap and release of the leash and a verbal correction, "No jump!

All Shelties like to jump up on people, but you can control this behavior by teaching your dog to sit.

ANTI-BARK COLLARS

There are a number of different anti-bark collars available commercially. There are collars triggered by barking that give the dog an electronic shock, collars that make a high-pitched noise, and ones that squirt a sniff of citronella. I am not a fan of the collars that shock the dog, especially for Shelties. I have seen dogs absolutely panic when corrected with those collars, often so badly that the dog screams (and the shock continues). However, the collar that makes a high-pitched sound and the collar that squirts citronella can both be very effective.

Photo by Isabelle Francais

Sit!" Of course, as with all of your training, praise him when he sits.

When you are out in public, make sure your Sheltie sits before any of your neighbors or friends pet him. Again, use your leash. If he won't sit still, don't let anyone pet him, even if you have to explain your actions, "I'm sorry, but I'm trying to teach him manners, and he must sit before he gets any petting."

The key to correcting jumping up is to make sure the bad behavior is not rewarded. If someone pets your Sheltie when he jumps up, that misbehavior has been rewarded. However, when he learns he only gets attention when he's sitting, that will make sitting more attractive to him.

Digging

If your backyard looks like a military artillery range, you need to concentrate first on preventing this problem from occurring. If you come home from work to find new holes in the lawn or garden, don't correct your dog then. He probably dug the holes when you first left in the morning, and a correction ten hours later won't work.

Instead, build him a dog run and leave him there during the day. If you fence off one side of your yard alongside your house, you might be able to give him a run that is 6 feet wide by 20 feet long. That's a great run. Let him trash this section to his heart's content; that's *his* yard.

Then when you are home and can supervise him, you can let him have free run of the rest of your yard. When he starts to get into trouble, you can use your voice to interrupt him, "Hey! What are you doing? Get out of the garden!"

The destructive dog also needs exercise, training, and playtime every day to use up his energy, stimulate his mind, and give him time with you.

Most importantly, don't let a dog that likes to dig watch you garden. If you do, he may come to you later with all of those bulbs you planted earlier!

Dashing Through Doors and Gates

This is actually one of the easier behavior problems to solve. Teach your Sheltie to sit at all doors and gates, then to hold that sit until you give him permission to go through or to get up after you have gone through. By teaching him to sit and wait for permission, you will eliminate the problem.

Start with your dog on the leash. Walk him up to a door. Have him sit, tell him to stay, and then open the door in front of him. If he dashes through, use the leash to correct him (snap and release) as you give him a verbal correction, "No! Stay!" Take him back to his original position and do it again. When he will hold it at this door, go to another door or gate and repeat the training procedure.

When he will wait (while on leash) at all doors and gates, take his leash off and hook up his long line. Fasten one end of the long line to a piece of heavy furniture. Walk him up to the door and tell him to sit and stay. Drop the long line to the ground. With your hands empty, open the door and stand aside. Because your hands are empty (meaning you aren't holding the leash), your Sheltie may decide to dash. If he does, the long line will stop him, or you can step on the line. Give him a verbal correction, too, "No! I said stay!" and bring him back to where he started. Repeat the training session here and at all other doors and gates.

Train your Sheltie to sit and wait for permission each time a door or gate is opened.

Photo by Isabelle Francais

RUNNING FREE

If your Sheltie does make it out through a door or gate, don't chase him. The more you chase, the better the game, as far as he's concerned. Instead, go get your shaker for teaching the come command. Shake it and say, "Sweetie, do you want a cookie? Come!" When he comes back to you, you must praise him for coming even though you may want to wring his neck for dashing through the door. Don't correct him—a correction will make him avoid you even more the next time it happens.

Other Problems?

Many behavior problems can be solved or at least controlled using similar techniques. Try to figure out why your Sheltie is doing what he's doing (from his point of view, not yours). What can you do to prevent the problem from happening? What can you do to teach your dog not to do it? Remember, as with all of your training, a correction alone will not change the behavior—you must also teach your dog what he can do.

If you still have some problems or if your dog is showing extreme fear, shyness, or aggressive tendencies, contact a dog trainer or behaviorist for some help.

Advanced
TRAINING
and Dog Sports

Shelties are bright, active dogs that would prefer to be doing something, anything, rather than living life as a couch potato. If you and your Sheltie enjoy your training and the time spent together during training, there is always more to do and learn. Teach him to listen to you off leash, teach him hand signals, and even some tricks. There is a lot you can do together, including a number of different dog activities and sports. Before you begin any of these exercises or activities, make sure your Sheltie is proficient in all of the basic commands. If he's not, go back and review and practice them.

When a Sheltie and his owner both enjoy training, there is no limit to what they can accomplish.

HAND SIGNALS

When you start teaching hand signals, use a treat in your hand to get your Sheltie's attention. Use the verbal command he already knows to help him understand what you are trying to tell him. As he responds, decrease the verbal command to a whisper and emphasize the hand signal.

The difficult part of teaching hand signals is that in the beginning, your dog may not understand that these movements of your hand and arm have any significance. After all, people "talk" with their hands all the time—hands are always moving and waving. Dogs learn early to ignore hand and arm movements. Therefore, to make hand signals work, your Sheltie needs to watch you. A

To learn a hand signal, your Sheltie must watch you.

USING HAND SIGNALS

Dog owners often think of hand signals as something that only really advanced dogs can respond to, and that is partly correct. It does take some training. However, hand signals are useful for all dog owners. For example, if your dog responds to hand signals, you can give him the signal to go lie down while you're talking on the telephone, and you won't have to interrupt your conversation to do so.

good treat in the hand that makes the movement can help.

Sit

If you were able to teach your Sheltie to sit using the treat above his nose, you were teaching him to sit using a hand signal. If you had to teach him by shaping him into a sit, you can still teach him a signal.

With your Sheltie on his leash, hold the leash in your left hand. Have a treat in your right hand. Stand in front of your Sheltie and take the treat from his nose upward. At the same time, whisper "Sit." When he

sits, praise him and release him. Try it again. When he is watching your hand and sitting reliably, stop whispering the command and let him follow the signal. If he doesn't sit, jiggle the leash and collar to remind him that something is expected. Again, when he sits, praise him.

Down

When you taught your Sheltie to lie down using the treat by taking the treat from his nose to the ground in front of his front paws, you were teaching him a hand signal. Granted, he was watching the treat in your hand, but he was also getting used to seeing your hand move. Therefore, switching him over from verbal command to a hand-signal-only command should be easy.

Have your dog sit in front of you. Verbally tell him, "Down" as you give him the hand signal for down (with a treat in your hand), just as you did when you were originally teaching it. When he lies down, praise him and then release him. Practice it a few times.

Now, give him the hand signal to go down (with a treat in your hand), but do not give a verbal command. If he lies down, praise him, give him the treat, and release him. If he does not go down, give the leash a slight snap and release down toward the ground—not hard, but just enough to let him know, "Hey! Pay attention!" When he goes down, praise and release him.

When he can reliably follow the signal with no verbal command, make it more challenging. Signal him to lie down when you are across the room from him, while you're talking to someone, and when there are some distractions around him. Remember to praise him enthusiastically when he goes down on the signal.

The hand signal for the stay command is the open-palmed gesture that your dog is already familiar with.

Stay

When you taught the stay command, you used a hand signal, the open-palmed gesture toward your Sheltie's face. This signal is so obvious your dog will probably do it without any additional training. Have your dog sit or lie down and tell him to "stay" using only the hand signal. Did he hold it? If he did, go back to him and praise him. If he didn't, use the leash to correct him (snap and release) and try it again.

Come

You want the signal to come to be a very broad, easily seen signal that your dog can recognize even if he's distracted by something. Therefore, this signal will be a wide swing of the right arm, starting with your arm held straight out to your side from the shoulder, horizontal to the ground. The motion will be to bring the hand to your chest following a wide wave—as if you were reaching out to get your dog and bring him to you.

Start teaching the signal by having the shaker you used to teach the come command in your right hand as you start the signal. Shake it slightly, just to get your dog's attention, and then complete the signal. Praise your dog when he responds and comes to you.

If he doesn't respond right away, start the signal again, and this time tell him (verbally) to come as you are making the signal and shaking the shaker. Again, praise him when he comes to you. Gradually eliminate the verbal command, and when your Sheltie is responding well, gradually stop using the shaker.

OFF-LEASH CONTROL

One of the biggest mistakes many dog owners make is to take the dog off the leash too soon. When you take your dog off the leash you have very little control—only your previous training can control your dog. If you take your dog off the leash before you have established enough control or before your dog is mentally mature enough to accept that control, you are setting yourself up for disaster.

Shelties are smart, curious

The signal for the come command is a wide gesture that starts with the arm outstretched and then sweeps toward the chest.

shetland sheepdog

Photo by Isabelle Francais

Don't let your Sheltie off leash in a public place until he is grown up and very well trained.

dogs, and they love to check out new things, especially new smells. A rabbit was made to chase as far as Shelties are concerned, and so was a butterfly or bird. More than one Sheltie has been so involved in his exploring that he's forgotten to pay attention to his owner's commands.

Before your Sheltie is to be allowed off leash (outside of a fenced yard or your backyard), you need to make sure your Sheltie's training is sound. This means he should be responding reliably and well to all of the basic commands.

Your Sheltie must also be mentally mature, and in some Shelties that might be a year-and-a-half to two years of age. He should be past the challenging teenage stage of development. Never take an adolescent off leash outside of a fenced-in area—that is asking for trouble.

Come on a Long Line

The long line (or leash) was introduced earlier in the section on teaching the come command. It is also a good training technique for preparing your dog for off-leash control. Review that section and practice the come command on the long line until you are comfortable your dog understands the come command from 20 to 30 feet

Photo by Isabelle Francais

Expect and demand the same level of obedience off leash that you do on leash. This includes heeling reliably.

shetland sheepdog

away (the length of the long line) and will do it reliably.

Now take him out to play in a different place that is still free from danger—a schoolyard is good. Let your Sheltie drag his long line behind him as you let him sniff and explore. When he's distracted and not paying attention to you, call him to come. If he responds right away, praise him enthusiastically. Tell him what a smart, wonderful dog he is.

If he doesn't respond right away, step on the end of the long line, pick it up, and back away from your dog, calling him again as you use the long line to make him come to you. Don't beg him to come to you or repeat the come command over and over. Simply use the line to *make* him do it. The come command is not optional.

Heel

Most public places require that dogs be leashed; however, teaching your Sheltie to heel without a leash is a good exercise. Not only is it a part of obedience competition (for people interested in that sport), but it's a good practical command, too. What would happen if your dog's leash or collar broke when you were out for a walk? Accidents happen,

and if your dog has already been trained to heel off leash, disaster would be averted!

To train for this, hook two leashes up to your dog's collar. Use your regular leash and a lightweight leash. Do a "watch me" exercise with treats, and then tell your dog to heel. Practice a variety of things; walk slowly, quickly, turn corners, and perform figure eights. When your dog is paying attention well, reach down and unhook his regular leash, tossing it to the ground in front of him. If he bounces up, assuming he's free, correct him with the second leash, "Hey! I didn't release you!" and make him sit in the heel position. Hook his regular leash back up and repeat the exercise.

When he doesn't take advantage of the regular leash being taken off, then tell him to heel and start practicing the heel. Do not use the second leash for minor correction but save it for control. If he tries to dash away, pull from you, or otherwise break the heel exercise, use the second leash and then hook his regular leash back on again.

Repeat this, going back and forth between one leash and two, until he's not even thinking about whether his regular leash

Conformation competitions can be a rewarding activity for show-quality Shelties and their owners.

is on or not. You want him to work reliably without questioning the leash's control. For some Shelties, this may take several weeks' worth of work.

When he is heeling reliably, put the second leash away. Take his regular leash, hook it to his collar and fold it up. Tuck it under his collar between his shoulder blades so that it is lying on his back. Practice his heel work. If he makes a mistake, grab the leash and collar as a handle and correct him. When the correction is over, take your hand off.

Expect and demand the same level of obedience off leash that you do on leash. Don't make excuses for off-leash work.

DOG SPORTS

Do you like training your Sheltie? If you and your Sheltie are having a good time, you may want to try one or more dog activities or sports. There are a lot of different things you can do with your dog. Some are competitive, some are fun, some are good works—what you decide to do depends on you and your dog.

Conformation Competition

The American Kennel Club (AKC) and the United Kennel Club (UKC) both award conformation championships to purebred dogs. The requirements vary between the registries, but basically, a

handsome, you might want to go watch a few local dog shows. Watch the Shelties competing and talk to some of the Sheltie owners and handlers. Does your Sheltie still look like a good candidate? You will also want to do some reading about your breed and conformation competition, or perhaps even attend a conformation class.

Obedience Competition

Obedience competition is a team sport involving you and your Sheltie. There are set exercises that must be performed in a certain way, and both you and your dog are judged as to your ability to perform these exercises.

Both the AKC and the UKC sponsor obedience competitions for all breeds of dog, as do some other organizations, including the American Shetland Sheepdog Association. There are also independent obedience competitions or tournaments held all over the country.

Whether or not your Sheltie is show-quality, you can make him look like he is. If you admire the fluffy, well-groomed look of show dogs, consider using a hair dryer on your dog after his bath. Photo courtesy of Metropolitan Vacuum Cleaner Co., Inc.

championship is awarded when a purebred dog competes against other dogs of his breed and wins. When competing, the judge compares each dog against a written standard for his breed and chooses the dog that most closely represents that standard of excellence.

This is a very simplistic explanation. However, if you feel your Sheltie is very

Before you begin training to compete, write to the sponsoring organization and get a copy of the rules and regulations pertaining to competitions. Go to a few local dog shows and watch the

Photo by Isabelle Francais

Shelties excel in fast-paced dog sports such as agility and flyball.

AGILITY
Agility is a fast-paced sport in which the dog must complete a series of obstacles correctly in a certain period of time, with the fastest time winning. Obstacles might include tunnels, hurdles, an elevated dog walk, and more. The AKC, the UKC, and the United States Dog Agility Association all sponsor agility competitions. Shelties are very fast, agile, and easily trained, and they do very well in agility competitions.

obedience competitions. See who wins and who doesn't. What did they do differently? There are also a number of books on the market specifically addressing obedience competition. You may want to find a trainer in your area who specializes in competition training.

Canine Good Citizen

The Canine Good Citizen (CGC) program was instituted by the AKC in an effort to promote and reward responsible dog ownership. During a CGC test, the dog and owner must complete a series of ten exercises, including sitting for petting and grooming, walking nicely on the leash, and the basic commands sit, down, stay, and come. On the successful completion of all ten exercises, the dog is awarded the title "CGC."

For more information about CGC tests, contact a dog trainer or dog training club in your area.

Temperament Test

The American Temperament Test Society was founded to provide breeders and trainers with a means of uniformly evaluating a dog's temperament. By using standardized tests, each dog would be tested in the same manner. The tests can be used to evaluate potential or future breeding stock, future working dogs, or simply as a way for dog owners to see how their dog might react in any given situation.

For information about temperament tests in your area, contact a local trainer or dog training club.

Herding

You don't need to have sheep in your backyard to be involved in herding as a sport. The American Kennel Club and several other organizations sponsor herding clinics and trials and offer herding titles to competing dogs. Although competitions are available for dogs working ducks, sheep, and cattle, Shelties usually don't work cattle. However, they are very proficient working ducks and sheep. Herding clinics and trials are a wonderful way to

If you wish to participate in competitions with your Sheltie, find a local instructor who specializes in that type of training.

Photo by Isabelle Francais

shetland sheepdog

see the breed's ancient instincts at work.

Therapy Dogs

Dog owners have known for years that our dogs are good for us, but now researchers are agreeing that dogs are good medicine. Therapy dogs go to nursing homes, hospitals, and children's centers to provide warmth, affection, and love to the people who need it most. Shelties make great therapy dogs. Contact your dog trainer or animal shelter for information about a group in your area.

FLYBALL

Flyball is a great sport for dogs that are crazy about tennis balls. Teams of four dogs and their owners compete against each other. The dogs—one per team at a time—run down the course, jump four hurdles, and trigger a mechanism that spits out a tennis ball. The dogs then catch the ball, turn, jump the four hurdles again, and return to their owner. The first team to complete the relay wins. Shetland Sheepdogs are very good retrievers, very fast, and easily trained, and do well in flyball competitions.

The sport of herding ducks and sheep comes naturally to Shelties. Clinics and trials demonstrate their ancient skill.

Photo by Judith E. Strom

shetland sheepdog

Have Some
FUN
With Your Training!

Training has a tendency to be serious—after all, much of training is teaching your Sheltie what his place in the family is and how to control himself. That can be serious stuff. However, training can be fun, especially from a Sheltie's viewpoint. Games and trick training can challenge your training skills and your Sheltie's ability to learn. Once you have taught your dog, though, you can have a great time showing off your dog's tricks, amusing your friends and just plain having fun with your dog.

RETRIEVING

Most Shelties like to retrieve, but they don't always understand the need to bring back what they go out after. However, once you teach your Sheltie to bring back the toy, retrieving games can be great fun as well as good exercise.

If your Sheltie likes to retrieve, then all you need to do is get him to bring you back the toy. When you throw the toy and he goes after it, wait until he picks it up. Once he has it in his mouth, call him back to you in a happy tone of voice. If he drops the toy, send him back to it. If he brings the toy all the way back to you, praise him enthusiastically.

Don't let him play tug-of-war with the toy. If he grabs it and doesn't want to let go, reach over the top of his muzzle and tell him "Give," as you press his top lips against his teeth. You don't have to use much pressure, just enough so that he opens his mouth to release the

If your Sheltie won't give you the toy he has retrieved, squeeze his muzzle gently.

Photo by Isabelle Francais

Photo by Judith E. Strom

This Sheltie loves his Frisbee®! If yours does, too, the two of you can have lots of fun.

FLYING DOGS

If your Sheltie likes to retrieve and is athletic (as most are), then teach him to retrieve a flying disc. Start by throwing the disc low for short distances. When he chases it, praise him. When he gets confident enough to jump for it, really praise him. As he gets braver and more skilled at the game, make the throws harder, higher, and longer—very gradually, of course, so you don't discourage him. Chasing and jumping after Frisbees® is a great game, lots of fun, and wonderful exercise.

toy. When he gives it to you, praise him.

If your Sheltie likes to take the toy and run with it, let him drag his long line behind him while he plays. Then, when he dashes off, you can step on the line and stop him. Once you've stopped him, call him back to you.

THE NAME GAME

The name game is a great way to make the dog think. And don't doubt for a minute that your Sheltie can think! When you teach your Sheltie the names of a variety of things around the house, you can then put him to work, too. Tell him to pick up your keys, your purse, or send him after the remote control to the television. The possibilities are unlimited.

Start with two items that are very different, perhaps a tennis ball and a magazine. Sit on the floor with your Sheltie and place the two items in front of you. Ask him, "Where's the ball?" and bounce the ball so that he tries to grab it or at least pays attention to it. When he touches it, praise him and give him a treat.

When he is responding to the ball, lay it on the floor and send him after it. Praise and reward him. Now set several different items out with the magazine and ball and send him after the

With practice, your dog can learn to retrieve his toys by name.

ball again. When he is doing well, start all over again with one of his toys. When he will get his toy, then put the toy and ball out there together and send him after one or the other. Don't correct him if he makes a mistake, just take the toy away from him and try it again. Remember, he's learning a foreign language (yours) at the same time that he's trying to figure out what the game is all about, so be patient.

FIND IT!

When the dog can identify a few items by name, you can start hiding those items so that he can search for them. For example, once he knows the word "keys" you can drop your keys on the floor under an end table next to the sofa. Tell your Sheltie, "Find my keys!" and help him look. Say, "Where are they?" and move him toward

Hide and seek can be a fun game for the whole family—including the dog.

Photo by Isabelle Francais

shetland sheepdog

the end table. When he finds them, praise him enthusiastically.

As he gets better, make the game more challenging. Make him search in more than one room. Have the item hiding in plain sight or underneath something else. Help him in the beginning when he appears confused. But don't let him give up—make sure he succeeds.

HIDE AND SEEK

Start by having a family member pet your Sheltie, offer him a treat, and then go to another room. Tell your Sheltie, "Find Dad!" and let him go. If he runs right to Dad, praise him! Have different family members play the game, and teach the dog a name for each of them so that he can search for each family member by name.

As he gets better at the game, the family member hiding will no longer have to pet the dog at the beginning of the game, he can simply go hide. Help your dog initially so that he can succeed, but encourage him, too, to use his nose and his scenting abilities.

SHAKE HANDS

Shaking hands is a very easy trick to teach. Have your dog sit in front of you. Reach behind

---

THE COME GAME FOR PUPPIES

Two family members can sit on the ground or floor across the yard or down the hallway from each other. Each should have some treats for the puppy. One family member calls the puppy across the yard or down the hall, and when the puppy reaches her, she praises the puppy and gives him a treat. She then turns the puppy around so that he's facing the other family member, who then calls the puppy. This very simple game can make teaching the come command exciting for the puppy. In addition, kids can play this game with the puppy, giving them a chance to participate in the puppy's training.

---

one front paw, and as you say, "Shake!" tickle his leg in the hollow just behind his paw. When he lifts his paw, shake it gently and praise him. When he starts lifting his paw on his own, stop the tickling.

WAVE

When your dog is shaking hands reliably, tell him, "Shake. Wave!" and instead of shaking his paw, reach toward it without taking it. Let him touch his paw to your hand, but pull your hand away so that he's waving. Praise him. Eventually, you want him to lift his paw

Photo by Isabelle Francais

Trick training is limited only by your imagination and your ability to train your Sheltie.

shetland sheepdog

higher than for the shake and to move it up and down so that he looks like he's waving. You can do that with the movements of your hand as he reaches for it. Praise him enthusiastically when he does it right. When he understands the wave, you can stop your hand movements.

Roll Over

With your Sheltie lying down, take a treat and make a

Photo by Isabelle Francais

Teaching your Sheltie to shake hands is very easy.

circle with your hand around his nose as you tell him, "Roll over." Use the treat (in the circular motion) to lead his head in the direction you want him to roll. Your other hand may have to help him.

HAVE FUN WITH TRICKS

I taught one of my dogs to play dead, and we both had a lot of fun with it. Michi got so good that he could pick the phrase "dead dog" out of casual conversation. One day the son of a neighbor of mine had just graduated from the police academy and was very proud of his new uniform. Michi and I were out front, so we went over to congratulate the new police officer. As I shook the police officer's hand, I turned to Michi and asked him, "Would you rather be a cop or a dead dog?" Michi dropped to the ground, went flat on his side, and closed his eyes. The only thing giving him away—that he really was having fun—was the wagging tail! Meanwhile, my neighbor's son was stuttering and turning red. He didn't know whether to be offended or to laugh. It was great fun!

MAKE UP YOUR OWN TRICKS

What would you and your Sheltie have fun doing? Teach him to stand up on his back legs and dance. Teach him to jump through a hula hoop or your arms forming a circle. Teach him to play dead or to sneeze. Trick training is limited only by your imagination and your ability to teach your dog.

SUGGESTED READING

BOOKS BY T.F.H. PUBLICATIONS

JG-109
Training the Perfect Puppy
Andrew DePrisco
160 pages, over 200 color photos

JG-117
A New Owner's Guide to
Dog Training
Dorman Pantfoeder
160 pages, over 100 full-color photos

TS-258
Training Your Dog for Sports and
Other Activities
Charlotte Schwartz
160 pages, 170 full-color photos

TS-283
Training Problem Dogs
Dr. Louis Vine
256 pages, 50 drawings